CRAFTCYCLE

100+ Eco-Friendly Projects and Ideas for Everyday Living

Heidi Boyd

NORTH LIGHT BOOKS
Cincinnati, Ohio

www.mycraftivity.com

13 12 11 10 09   5 4 3 2 1

Distributed in Canada by Fraser Direct
100 Armstrong Avenue
Georgetown, ON, Canada L7G 5S4
Tel: (905) 877-4411

Distributed in the U.K. and Europe by David & Charles
Brunel House, Newton Abbot, Devon, TQ12 4PU, England
Tel: (+44) 1626 323200, Fax: (+44) 1626 323319
E-mail: postmaster@davidandcharles.co.uk

Distributed in Australia by Capricorn Link
P.O. Box 704, S. Windsor NSW, 2756 Australia
Tel: (02) 4577-3555

Library of Congress Cataloging-in-Publication Data
Boyd, Heidi Craftcycle : 100+ eco-friendly projects and ideas for everyday living / by Heidi Boyd. –1st ed.
    p. cm.
Includes index.
ISBN-13: 978-1-60061-304-3 (pbk. : alk. paper)
ISBN-10: 1-60061-304-7 (pbk. : alk. paper)
1. Handicraft. 2. Recycling (Waste, etc.) I. Title.
TT157.B715 2009
745.5–dc22
                                    2009008575

THE PAGES OF THIS BOOK ARE PRINTED ON 60% Post-Consumer Recycled Paper.

Development Editor: Jessica Gordon
Content Editor: Jolie Lamping Roth
Production Editor: Vanessa Lyman
Designer: Geoff Raker
Production Coordinator: Greg Nock
Photographer: Ric Deliantoni
Photo Stylist: Nora Martini
Step-By-Step Illustrations: Heidi Boyd
Building Diagrams: Jon Boyd

Metric Conversion Chart

to convert	to	multiply by
Inches	Centimeters	2.54
Centimeters	Inches	0.4
Feet	Centimeters	30.5
Centimeters	Feet	0.03
Yards	Meters	0.9
Meters	Yards	1.1
Sq. Inches	Sq. Centimeters	6.45
Sq. Centimeters	Sq. Inches	0.16
Sq. Feet	Sq. Meters	0.09
Sq. Meters	Sq. Feet	10.8
Sq. Yards	Sq. Meters	0.8
Sq. Meters	Sq. Yards	1.2
Pounds	Kilograms	0.45
Kilograms	Pounds	2.2
Ounces	Grams	28.3
Grams	Ounces	0.035

Cooking Conversion Chart

U.S. Units	Metric Units
¼ teaspoon	1 milliliters
½ teaspoon	2 milliliters
1 teaspoon	5 milliliters
½ tablespoon	7 milliliters
¾ tablespoon	11 milliliters
1 tablespoon	15 milliliters
¼ cup	60 milliliters
⅓ cup	80 milliliters
½ cup	125 milliliters
⅔ cup	160 milliliters
1 cup	250 milliliters
1 quart	1 liter
1 fluid ounce	30 milliliters
1 ounce	30 grams
½ pound	225 grams
1 pound	455 grams

Temperature Conversion Chart

Fahrenheit	Celsius
300°	150°
325°	160°
350°	180°
450°	230°

NOTE: The metric units and Celsius degrees given are estimates, not exact measurements.

fw media
www.fwmedia.com

Heidi Boyd

About the Author

Heidi Boyd is the author of ten books with North Light Books, most notably the Simply Beautiful series. She crafts at the dining table, where she can keep an eye on the family and dash out the door for the next carpool. Her goal is to make sophisticated design approachable and easy for all. She has a fine arts degree and got her start in professional crafting as a contributor to Better Homes and Gardens books and magazines. Her husband, Jon Boyd, has been helping behind the scenes with many book projects. He is a LEED-accredited, licensed architect with twenty years of commercial and residential design experience. This is the first time he's contributed designs, drawings and projects of his own. Together, Heidi and Jon and their three children actively enjoy the natural beauty of their midcoast Maine home.

Check out Heidi's blog on www.mycraftivity.com.

Dedication
This book is dedicated with love to our children, Jasper, Elliot and Celia. We wish you a beautiful green world.

Acknowledgments

A project this size requires the efforts and enthusiasm of many. I'm fortunate to be surrounded by talented and generous friends. I owe a debt of gratitude to my good friend Hannah Beattie, who lent her sewing expertise to the book, and her husband, Bart, for the amazing potting bench project. A big thank-you to knitting designer Chesley Flotten for the fabulous afghan, Catherine Matthews Scanlon for her ingenious tin can pincushions, Rose Nelson's garden digs and camera talents, Tony DiPietro for graciously allowing us to photograph some of his extraordinary birdhouses, and my wonderful neighbor Claudia Brzoza, who generously shared both her treasure trove of recycled goods and words of encouragement.

Contents

Chapter 1

Chapter 2

Chapter 3

Chapter 4

Intro

Creativity and being green go hand in hand. Resourceful artists have been reusing available materials to make stunning works of art since before recorded history. Museums are filled with examples of useful and beautiful handicrafts made with castoffs. Native Americans made stunning patterns with natural plant dyes on buffalo hide to create beautiful, functional bags they called *parfleche*. Gorgeous early American quilts were elaborately pieced with clothing scraps, and some even reveal stories of the Underground Railroad. In our modern society, we're programmed to go to the stores and buy what we need. Most of us would never think of stitching our own suitcase or bed covers. Our economy is almost completely based on consumerism. The majority of our waste comes from the packaging and disposal of these goods.

The first step of craft cycle is to get you to look at what we dispose of with heightened awareness. You might be surprised by the wealth of creative materials that is within your reach. The common by-products of our consumerism lifestyle such as plastic bags, food packaging, cardboard boxes, worn clothing, plastic bottles, and even bike inner tubes are excellent crafting materials. Only, these highly manufactured items often require more than a simple dot of glue or stitch to assemble them into new creations. I found that with a few simple modifications and handy tips, many of the classic crafting techniques such as cutting, folding, ironing, sewing, knitting and crocheting also work well with most of these nontraditional materials.

A huge amount of satisfaction comes from making something beautiful and functional out of what many consider waste. Who would have known that potato chip bags could fold into a neat little purse, or that a stack of well-worn T-shirts would hook into an attractive shaggy rug? Whenever I shared a work-in-progress for this book, the enthusiasm was infectious. I found that craft cycling also helps build neighborhoods and communities. Once people heard what I was doing, teachers placed chip bags in my daughter's preschool cubby, and neighbors dropped plastic lids in my mailbox.

Creating out of waste is one effective way of reducing your carbon footprint, and maybe that of your friends and neighbors, too. There are so many other small and easy ways that we can help our planet. The foods we eat, the way we live in our homes and how we commute all impact the environment. We've intentionally arranged this book into four seasons so that you can quickly find appropriate craftcycling projects that integrate organizational finds in the spring, that feature natural materials in the summer, that highlight back-to-school supplies and apartment furnishings in the fall and that offer plenty of gift ideas in the winter. In each season, you'll also find our tried-and-true family favorite recipes that will encourage you to eat wonderfully fresh, locally grown food. Jon lent his expertise to build the large-scale projects and help me compile easy and green living tips to maximize your home's efficiency and help us tread lightly on our precious world.

Being green and being creative has never been more exciting and fun!

7

Chapter 1
spring

Spring has sprung! Open your home to fresh, warm breezes and get your spring cleaning started. When you place winter clothes in storage, take the time to sort outgrown and worn clothes. Pile up old jeans, pj's, T-shirts, odd socks and sheets. You'll be surprised how easy it is to transform them into rugs, quilts, toys and hampers to brighten your home. Don't worry if the fabric has stains, rips or worn patches. It's easy to cut away those areas and salvage the best parts to use in your creation. You don't need to be a seamstress or expert knitter to make any of these projects. The steps are simple, and you'll be knitting, hooking or stitching in no time.

When you sweep under the carpets, you might discover a new collection of odds and ends to add to an already growing basket of children's toy pieces. You may also have a game or two that no one plays with because it's missing pieces. Don't throw these interesting bits and pieces into the trash. They're fabulous for fusing into bowls or setting in resin for one-of-a-kind serving trays. You'll even find instructions in this chapter for wiring together old slides into a lampshade.

Spring takes its sweet time to get to Maine, and when it finally arrives, we are extremely happy to greet it. The warm air and tender buds hold the promise of a new growing season. It's time to get your garden jump-started with the help of our clever cold frame. It repurposes an old window sash to insulate delicate new shoots from cold winter nights. Recycled wood is also the perfect building material for birdhouses. Take inspiration from Tony DiPietro's clever homes. It's the perfect time to encourage nesting birds into your yard.

 What a Green Idea!

Work off the winter blahs! Spring is calling, so dust off those bike pedals, tune up your bike and ride on!

Find more springtime activities in *Living the Green Life* on pages 36–37.

Hooked T-Shirt Rug

WHEN I WAS little, I used to love choosing boxed rug hooking kits from the hobby store. I was thrilled to see how well the hooking technique transferred from yarn to T-shirt strips. The tension from looping the strips in place causes the strips to form attractive curled ends. This shaggy rug came together relatively quickly—the thick T-shirt strips fill up the canvas so you only have to hook every other row. Old T-shirts are so plentiful you shouldn't have trouble finding a wide selection of colors. In my house, with three males, worn white T-shirts are readily available. A rotary cutter, cutting mat and clear ruler help me quickly slice the shirts into piles of strips.

What a Green Idea!

When you start spring cleaning, remember old T-shirts make great cleaning rags. Check your kitchen cabinets for biofriendly cleaning supplies, like baking soda. Baking soda brightens chrome taps, removes coffee stains from countertops, deodorizes and cleans the inside of the fridge and removes mildew from the bathtub.

Find more seasonal ideas in *Living the Green Life* on pages 36–37.

Materials List

RECYCLED MATERIALS

Assorted colored T-shirts, one each of: kelly green, olive green, teal, orange, light pink, dark pink, fuchsia, yellow
Generous stack of white undershirts and T-shirts

OTHER MATERIALS

24" × 38" (61cm × 97cm) rug hooking canvas

TOOLS & SUPPLIES

Rotary cutter, clear ruler and self-healing mat
Duct tape
Rug hooking tool
Thin string and darning needle

RESOURCES

Finished size: 20" × 33" (51cm × 84cm)

Step 1 Working over cutting mat, use rotary cutter to remove T-shirt's sleeves, shoulder seams and hem edge so that you're left with smooth, seamless fabric.

Step 2 Using ruler as a straightedge, cut the shirt into two 7" (18cm) sections. You'll get just one section out of a child's shirt and up to three sections out of an adult's shirt.

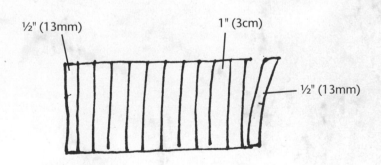

½" (13mm)   1" (3cm)

½" (13mm)

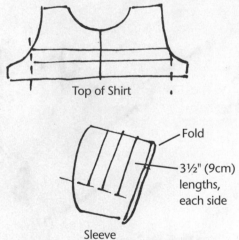

Top of Shirt

Fold

3½" (9cm) lengths, each side

Sleeve

Step 3 Stack the two 7" (18cm) sections over each other and cut through the thickness to divide the fabric into 1" (3cm) sections. Take the side fold into consideration, and cut the first and last strips ½" (13mm) from the outside edge. When they unfold, they'll be an inch in width.

Step 4 You can salvage more 1" × 7" (3cm × 18cm) strips by cutting horizontal strips from the top of the shirt and folded strips from the sleeves. Cut the remaining shirts, grouping the piles by color so they're ready for hooking. Leave the white shirts for last. You'll be better able to gauge how many you'll need after hooking the colored sections of your rug.

MORE STEPS ↪

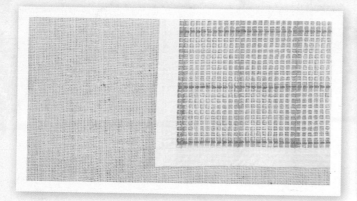

Step 5 Cover all four edges of the canvas with tape. Place the raw canvas edge halfway across a length of tape, then fold the tape over the top, trapping the canvas edge inside the tape. This will protect it from unraveling and be more comfortable to work with.

Step 6 Thread the hooking tool through the canvas where you want to place the first strip. The tip should sit on top of the canvas and the selected canvas bar will lie over the tool. Fold a T-shirt strip in half and hook it onto the tool. Pull the tool back down through the canvas, bringing the loop halfway out the canvas.

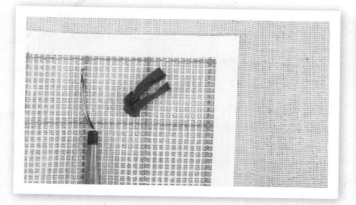

Step 7 Use your fingers to push the ends through the loop, then pull the ends up to tighten the knot. Repeat the process to add strips to every other canvas square.

Step 8 Continue adding the same colored strips until you've created a square or rectangle. Switch to a contrasting color and surround your shape with a one- or two-row border. Repeat the shape and border one to two more times in other locations on the canvas. Using all your remaining colored strips, create large and small framed square and rectangle combinations and distribute them over the canvas. Fill in all the blank canvas areas with white T-shirt strips.

Step 9 Carefully remove the tape on one side of the rug, then fold the raw edge in half and then flat against the underside of the rug. The raw edge is now trapped in the fold. Using a length of lightweight string and a darning needle, stitch the folded edge in place. Repeat for the remaining sides, removing each section of tape just before you're ready to sew.

Tin Can Sewing Caddy & Pincushion

Catherine Matthews Scanlon designed this lovely piece; she came up with the idea when she was cleaning out a can for recycling. She realized the can could not only make a good base for a pin cushion, but it also would make a handy storage container for a small pair of scissors, spool of thread and thimble. She covered the cans with scrapbook paper scraps and beautiful vintage buttons. I stitched together the pincushion tops with two circles of felted sweater scraps.

Materials List

RECYCLED MATERIALS
Aluminum can
Scraps of patterned papers
Buttons
Measuring tape
Felted sweater scraps

OTHER MATERIALS
Stuffing
Chenille, cord or rickrack trims

TOOLS & SUPPLIES
Metal file (if necessary)
Double-sided tape
Glue gun and glue sticks
Sewing needle and thread, or
    sewing machine

RESOURCES
Project Note: page 114

Step 1 Carefully remove and discard the lid of tin can. Use a metal file to smooth any sharp edges. We've found that not all can openers are created equal. Catherine's hand-cranked opener prepared these cans. I have a very similar model, but it leaves a jagged edge. Make sure you completely clean and dry the empty can before crafting.

Step 2 Trim decorative paper to the length of the can, making sure it fits between the top and bottom rims. Use strips of double-sided tape to affix the paper around the outside of the can. Hot glue buttons or a section of measuring tape around the outside of the can.

Step 3 Trace a circle that extends a ½" (13mm) beyond the circumference of the can. Cut two circles of this size out of a felted sweater. Pin the circles right sides together. If you're using upholstery cording, position it between the layers before pinning. Machine or hand stitch the edges together, leaving a 1" (3cm) opening to turn the piece right side out. Tightly pack the pincushion with stuffing, then hand stitch the opening closed. If you're trimming the piece with chenille, cord or rickrack, hot glue it around the seam. The trims not only look pretty, they also support the pincushion on top of the can.

If you have children in your home, you may be constantly surprised by the flotsam and jetsam that ends up on your counter or in your dustpan. This project is the perfect way to turn all those odds and ends into a functional piece of art. A game board, LEGO pieces, dominos and playing cards make a wonderful collage that comes together with two layers of poured cast resin. This project could just as easily be made with hairpins, barrettes and costume jewelry to make a lovely tray for a vanity. Sewing patterns, buttons, pins, measuring tapes and snaps gather for a beautiful sewing-themed tray.

Games-to-Play Serving Tray

Materials List

RECYCLED MATERIALS
Game board
Playing cards
Puzzle pieces
Game pieces
Poker chips
K'NEX and LEGO pieces
Jacks
Dice
Plastic animals

OTHER MATERIALS
Serving tray (be sure the handle openings are raised above the serving surface so that there's room to pour the resin.)
Mini marbles

TOOLS & SUPPLIES
Aleene's Tacky Glue
Glossy Accents
Adhesive brush
Aleene's Platinum Bond Glass and Bead Adhesive
Crystal Clear Glaze Coat (Famowood)
Plastic containers (for mixing the resin solution)
Wax paper
Rubber gloves
Plastic spoon and knife
Toothpicks

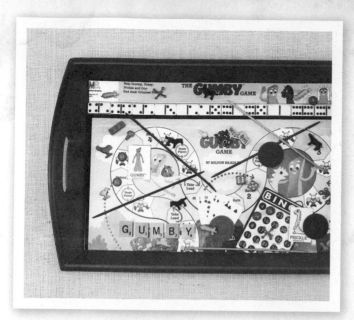

Step 1 Play with the pieces on your tray to find an arrangement you like. Remove the pieces and begin by gluing the biggest pieces down. Use Tacky Glue for game board and paper pieces, and brush on a protective coat of Glossy Accents. After the coat has dried, use Platinum Bond to attach the plastic and metal pieces. Let the glue set for 24 hours before pouring on the resin.

Step 2 Work in a well-ventilated area. Lay down wax paper to protect your worktable, and pull on rubber gloves. Carefully mix half the resin solution according to package directions. This will give you approximately ¼" (6mm) thickness. Quickly spread the resin over the tray. Use a plastic knife to help spread the solution over pieces. Sprinkle in mini marbles. Use a toothpick to adjust anything in the resin. If the bubbles don't disperse quickly, you can use the toothpick to pop them, or gently exhale hot air directly over the surface. (Caution: Do not inhale!) Make these alterations quickly as you don't want to agitate the surface as it begins to cure. Anything that isn't glued in place may shift while the resin self levels.

Tip
Select low-profile pieces for your tray. The higher the profile, the more resin you'll need to cover them.

Step 3 After 72 hours, your tray should be fully cured. Some higher-profile pieces may need another ¼" (6mm) of resin to cover them. If necessary, glue any new thin pieces to the cured surface and let them dry overnight. Repeat the pouring process from Step 2 to add another layer of resin.

Oh boy, is this project a blast! I had so much fun melting these little guys together, and the result is nothing short of impressive! Don't let any plastic men or animals collect dust in a box. It's time to break them out and turn them into a cool centerpiece. My one concern in making this project was the potential off-gassing of the melting plastic. I worked outside and was careful to heat only contact areas. The craft heat gun wasn't too hot, and the residual heat was trapped in the metal bowl, which helped bend the plastic with slow and steady warmth. I found the fumes to be very minimal. I would agree it's not the greenest project, but it is creative recycling and does reuse plastic.

Toy Figure Bowl

Safety Reminders

Melting plastic emits fumes. Be sure to work in a well-ventilated area and heat only the contact areas.

The heat gun will warm the metal bowl, which conducts the heat. Be careful not to burn yourself when handling the heated bowl.

Materials List

RECYCLED MATERIALS
Approximately 100 plastic figures

TOOLS & SUPPLIES
Large metal bowl 4" × 11½" (10cm × 29cm)
Heat gun
Metal spoon or craft stick

RESOURCES
Finished size: 7"–8" × 11"
   (18cm–20cm × 28cm)

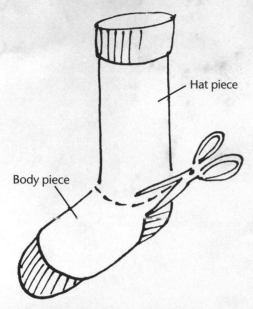

Hat piece

Body piece

Step 1 Select the sock for the baby's body. It's best if you can use one that has little wear in the toe. Cut off the top of the sock just above the heel. Save the top part of the sock for the hat.

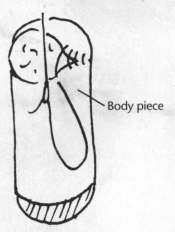

Body piece

Step 2 Generously fill the toe portion of the sock with fiberfill. Pull the heel over the top of the opening and hand sew it closed. This will form the top of your sock baby head.

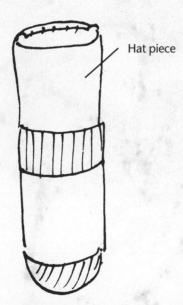

Hat piece

Step 3 Use either the saved top of the sock or the top of another sock for the baby's hat. Pull it cuff first over the baby's head. Fold over and hand stitch the top cut edge to prevent it from unraveling.

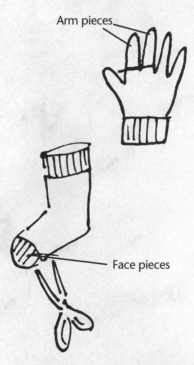

Arm pieces

Face pieces

Step 4 Cut the toe off a toddler sock for the baby's face and two fingers off a knit glove for the baby's arms. Turn the fingers inside out. Stuff all three pieces with fiberfill.

MORE STEPS

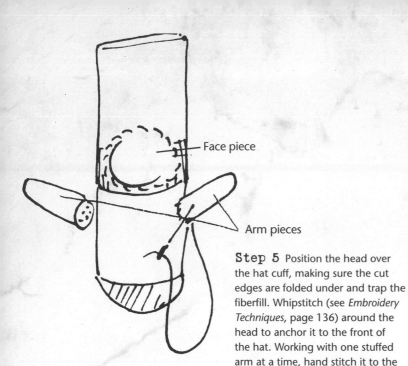

Face piece

Arm pieces

Step 5 Position the head over the hat cuff, making sure the cut edges are folded under and trap the fiberfill. Whipstitch (see *Embroidery Techniques*, page 136) around the head to anchor it to the front of the hat. Working with one stuffed arm at a time, hand stitch it to the side of the body. Be careful to catch loose knitted stitches along the cut edge with your sewing needle to prevent them from unraveling.

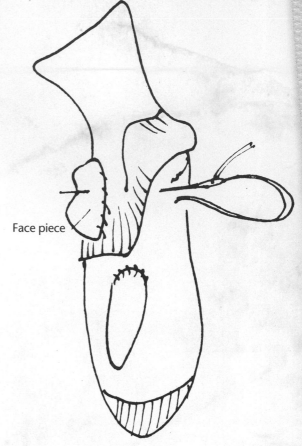

Face piece

Step 6 Flip up the back of the hat. With a darning needle threaded with a full six strands of embroidery floss, make a stitch from the back of the baby's head up through the center of its face. Make a French knot (see *Embroidery Techniques*, page 137) for a nose and then stitch back through to the back of the head and pull tight. Repeat the process to create two eyes above the nose. Once you've knotted the embroidery thread and trimmed the end, fold the hat back down.

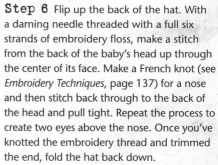

Step 7 Gather the top of the baby's hat together and cinch it with a few stitches for a younger child, or tie a ribbon around it for a child over three. Use the top of another sock to make a playful blanket pouch. Hand stitch the cut bottom edge closed and slip the finished sock baby inside.

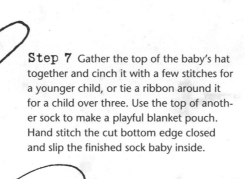

Top of another sock

If you've replaced your record collection with compact discs and MP3 files, consider melting your heavily scratched records and turning them into useful home decor. My sixteen-year-old son actually stayed in the kitchen to help with this project; it intrigued him. It's easy to see why. The project has a quick, easy process with instant results. The trick is to keep your eye on the melting record and when it starts to droop, immediately pull it from the oven and shape it in a waiting ceramic bowl.

Groovy Record Bowl

Materials List

RECYCLED MATERIALS
Vinyl record

TOOLS & SUPPLIES
7" (18cm) diameter metal mixing bowl
9" (23cm) diameter ceramic mixing bowl
Metal cookie tray
Oven mitts

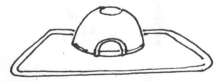

Step 1 Lower the top oven rack to the middle position and preheat the oven to 300°F (150°C). Open a window in the room to increase ventilation.

Invert a metal bowl and place it in the center of a cookie sheet. Place it in the oven so that it's prewarmed. Have a ceramic bowl ready for use on your counter.

Step 2 Clean both sides of a vinyl record with water and dry it with a lint-free towel. Carefully place the record over the inverted bowl, centering the record label over the middle of the bowl. Place them in the oven for just a few minutes. Pull on your oven mitts so you're ready for the next step.

Step 3 Keep a close eye on the oven; in minutes, the sides of the album will begin to droop. Immediately snatch the album out of the oven and press it firmly into the ceramic bowl. Quickly ripple the edges and press the folds flat against the sides of the bowl. You don't have time to hesitate. The record cools almost instantly. Once it's no longer pliable, pop it out of the bowl and it will hold its new shape.

The inspiration for this hamper came from traditional coiled baskets. It's a no-sew project. The strips of pajamas are simply wrapped around a thick rope, and the wrapped rope is coiled into a spiral. The pajama strips intermittently wrap around two thicknesses of rope to attach each new coil to the spiral. Dabs of hot glue secure the strip ends. This project is easy enough for children to help with, and just the thing to keep their rooms organized.

Coiled Pajama Laundry Basket

What a Green Idea!

Laundry accounts for 25 percent of a home's hot water costs. To be more energy efficient, make sure loads are full, but don't overload your machine. Use warm or cold water for washing, if appropriate, and cold water for the rinse cycle. Use dryer stones instead of chemically treated fabric softeners.

Find more seasonal ideas in *Living the Green Life* on pages 36–37.

Materials List

RECYCLED MATERIALS
4-5 adult-sized knit pajama bottoms

OTHER MATERIALS
Approximately 150' (46m) of ¼" (6mm) rope (use whatever you have on hand, just make sure it's completely dry)

TOOLS & SUPPLIES
Scissors
Glue gun and glue sticks

RESOURCES
Finished size: 15" × 12" (38cm × 30cm)

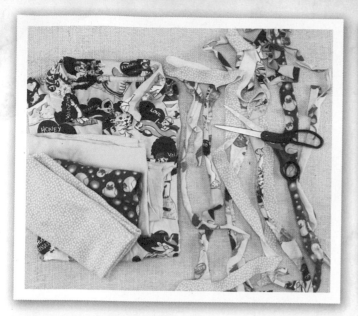

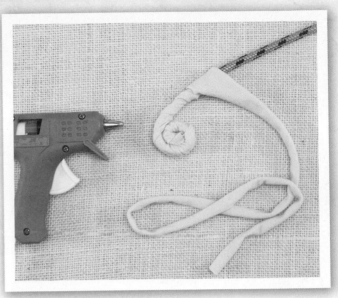

Step 1 Cut the waist elastic, pockets and leg hems off the pajama bottoms. Cut the pajamas into 1" (3cm) vertical strips.

Step 2 To begin the coil, hot glue the end of a pajama strip to the end of the rope. Wrap the strip around the rope about nine times, making sure that the fabric lays flat and smooth. Form the end of the wrapped rope into a tight spiral, and use a few drops of hot glue to anchor it in place.

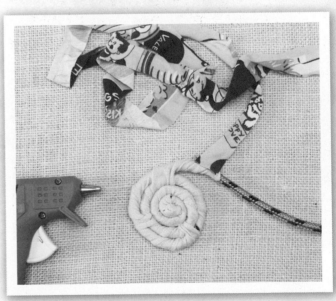

Step 3 To build on this beginning, you'll need to connect the newly wrapped rope to the coil by looping the pajama strip around the coil directly beneath it. Wrap the rope three more times and then repeat the looping. Be sure the rope is completely concealed in fabric before and after the strip loops through the coil.

Step 4 When you run out of fabric, hot glue another strip over the end and continue wrapping, coiling and looping. Try to distribute different prints and colors throughout the hamper.

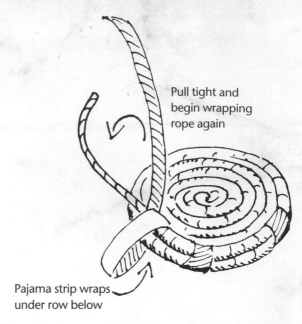

Pull tight and begin wrapping rope again

Pajama strip wraps under row below

Step 5 When your coil reaches 12" (30cm) in diameter, begin stacking the newly wrapped rope over the last row. This marks the transition to building up the sides of the hamper.

Step 6 Use the same wrapping technique to layer the rope on top of itself to create and build the sides.

Step 7 Once your hamper is 11" (28cm) high, you need to work handles into the top. To do this, simply wrap the fabric strip that your working with around 5" (13cm) of the rope without passing the fabric strip into the coiled sides. Return to the established pattern, stopping to make another 5" (13cm) wrapped rope section on the opposite side of the basket. From here on, continue wrapping and coiling until you've made six rows above your handle.

Step 8 Once you've reached the end, cut off the rope. Then trim the fabric strip ¼" (6mm) from the end of the rope and glue the fabric strip over the rope end.

Fruit Net
Pot Scrubbers

If you've ever been gifted a scrubbie from a grandma, you know how well this old-time craft cleans. Making your own out of salvaged net produce bags is a quick little project. Not only does it save a handy material from the garbage, it also cleans a mountain of dishes. You can save the ends of your bar soap and tuck them into a piece of netting. All those pieces will quickly add up to a new bar. The netting holds them together, while letting the water and suds wash away.

Materials List

RECYCLED MATERIALS
Net produce bags

TOOLS & SUPPLIES
Scissors
Size L crochet hook

RESOURCES
Crochet Techniques: pages 134–135

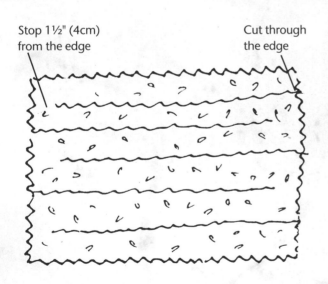

Stop 1½" (4cm) from the edge

Cut through the edge

Step 1 Use scissors to cut off any metal staples or labels on the bags. Make a vertical slit up the side of the bag and flatten it. Cut the bag into a single 1" (3cm) strip, as shown in the illustration. By not cutting through to the end, the strip stays connected.

Step 2 Use the following pattern to crochet the scrubber (see *Crochet Techniques,* pages 134–135):

a.) Chain 3 stitches. Make a single crochet to connect it into a loop

b.) Double crochet 12 stitches around the loop.

c.) Double crochet into each stitch for a total of 13 stitches.

d.) Change colors. Double crochet in the first stitch. Make 2 double crochets in the next stitch. Repeat alternation until you've encircled the scrubber.

e.) Pull the end up through the last stitch. Trim it and weave it into your work.

You can't appreciate the best part of this project simply by looking at the photograph. Its greatest quality is how wonderful the rug feels under your feet. I've been chasing my kids off it to keep it fresh for the photo shoot. It's the perfect rug to place by your bed and step onto every morning. Once you've cut old sheets into a continuous strip, the knitting part is a cinch. It requires giant needles and is a perfect beginner knitting project. The whole rug is knitted in garter stitch so it lays flat on the floor.

Knitted Linens Rug

What a Green Idea!

Declutter your home and find new homes for your unwanted goods. Bring clothes, bedding and household goods to Goodwill (www.goodwill.org) or Salvation Army (www.salvationarmyusa.org).

Find more seasonal ideas in *Living the Green Life* on pages 36–37.

Materials List

RECYCLED MATERIALS
Assorted color sheets: brown, turquoise, white, green

TOOLS & SUPPLIES
Scissors
17mm knitting needles

RESOURCES
Knitting Techniques: pages 130–133
Finished Size: 25" × 38" (63cm × 96cm)

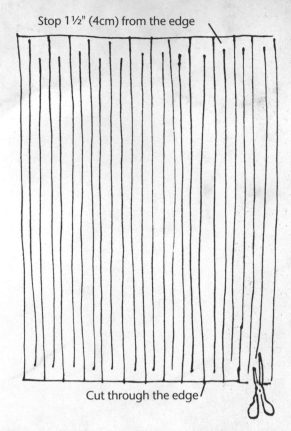

Stop 1½" (4cm) from the edge

Cut through the edge

Step 1 Spread a sheet flat on a large table or the floor. With scissors, remove all the hems so you're left with a single thickness of fabric. Begin cutting the sheet into 1" (3cm) strips. To make a continuous strip, follow the diagram above and stop your cuts 1½" (4cm) from the edge. Begin each new cut from the outside edge.

Step 2 Once you're finished cutting, begin rolling your new fabric yarn into a ball. The larger turning sections will create bulk and add interest to your work. Repeat the process with the remaining sheets until you have several balls of different colors ready to knit.

Step 3 Use the following pattern to knit the rug (see *Knitting Techniques*, pages 130–133):

a.) Cast on 50 stitches in green.

b.) Garter stitch 7 rows.

c.) Change to brown and garter stitch 11 rows.

d.) Change to turquoise and garter stitch 3 rows.

e.) Change to green and garter stitch 2 rows.

f.) Change to white and garter stitch 15 rows.

g.) Change to brown and garter stitch 3 rows.

h.) Change to green and garter stitch 2 rows.

i.) Change to turquoise and garter stitch 11 rows.

j.) Change to white and garter stitch 7 rows.

k.) Change to green and garter stitch 5 rows.

l.) Change to brown and garter stitch 17 rows.

m.) Change to white and garter stitch 5 rows.

n.) Change to turquoise and garter stitch 5 rows.

o.) Bind off.

If you have a box of old slides sitting in the attic or taking up space in a closet, this project is for you. By simply drilling holes in the corners of the slides, you can easily stitch them together with wire. Four sheets of connected slides are then looped onto an old lampshade frame. This recycled lamp makes as fabulous a centerpiece as it does a beautiful frame for forgotten images.

Materials List

RECYCLED MATERIALS
Lamp and old shade
Slides in plastic mounts

TOOLS & SUPPLIES
24-gauge black-and-white wire (Fun Wire)
Drill with ⅛" (3mm) drill bit
Wire cutters

RESOURCES
Project Note: twenty-one slides cover each side of my shade, for a total of 84.
Finished lampshade: 12¼" × 6" (31cm × 15cm) square

Slide Lampshade

Step 1 Stack four to five slides together; make sure they're all oriented the same way. Drill a hole in each corner. Repeat the process to prepare the remaining slides. (These slides are placed flat for illustration purposes.)

Step 2 Line up the slides on your work surface, orienting them the same way, printed side up, and distributing colors and patterns throughout the rows. Connections are made at the corners where four slides meet. Begin making a cross-stitch between these slides. To do this, thread a 4" (10cm) section of wire down through the top left slide then up through top right slide next to it.

Step 3 Bring the wire diagonally down through the lower left slide, then bring it up through the lower right slide. Carefully remove any slack while still permitting the slides to lay flat.

Step 4 Twist the wire ends from the top left and bottom right together and trim the ends. Continue joining slides in this fashion to connect all the slides onto a shade. To complete the shape, you'll need to bend the corner connections and reach inside to join the first and last rows together.

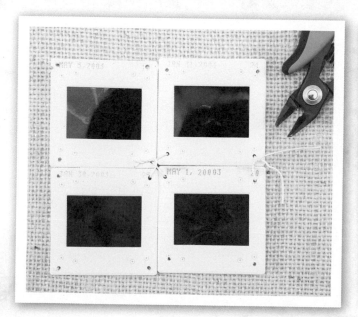

Step 5 The top and bottom edges of the shade are a series of two slides connected by a single stitch. Twist these wires together, leaving them untrimmed so that they can hang the finished shade onto the frame.

Step 6 If necessary, remove the existing paper shade. Save the collar, top and bottom frames. Paint or wrap them with wire. To hang the finished shade from the prepared wires, separate the white wire ends and place them on either side of the frame. Twist them together at the top of the frame.

This quilt is beautiful enough to hang on the wall, but sturdy enough to travel with and lay on the floor for a baby to play on. The jean panels are salvaged dungarees, whose sturdy weight handles embroidery stitches without pulling or puckering. The filling is layered flannel sheets, and the backing is a salvaged curtain panel. Brighten your design with bright calico pieces or sections of cotton clothing. The layers are simply knotted together at the panel corners.

A big thank-you to Hannah Beattie, who helped me finish this piece. I love embroidery and playing with the colors and fabrics, but squaring up corners and figuring out borders is foreign to me!

Denim Quilt

Tip
If you are buying fabric, whenever possible look for organic cotton, fair trade material made in safe working environments and shot gun cotton that uses less harmful dyes.

Materials List

RECYCLED MATERIALS
One pair of jeans
Cotton fabric scraps at least 18" (46 cm) wide, in four colors: three ¼-yard (23cm) long and one ½-yard (46cm) long
½ yard (46cm) corduroy scrap
Salvaged curtain backing, or purchased fabric

OTHER MATERIALS
Flannel sheet batting, or purchased batting
Embroidery thread: yellow, red, orange, ochre, light pink, dark pink, purple, blue, turquoise, green, white

TOOLS & SUPPLIES
Rotary cutter, clear ruler and self-healing mat
Scissors
Embroidery hoop
Sewing machine
Straight pins
Darning needle
Sewing needles

RESOURCES
Embroidery Techniques: pages 136–137
Patterns: pages 138–139

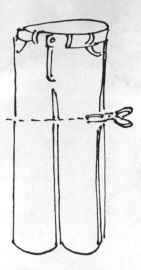

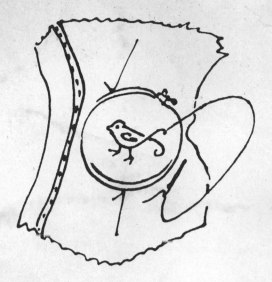

Step 1 Lay the jeans flat on your work surface and cut off the least worn leg section—often the back will be darker than the front. Cut one of the side seams open so the denim unfolds into a flat piece of fabric

Step 2 Trap the denim in an embroidery hoop, pulling any slack tight before twisting the clamp. See step 3 to embroider a bird or snail.

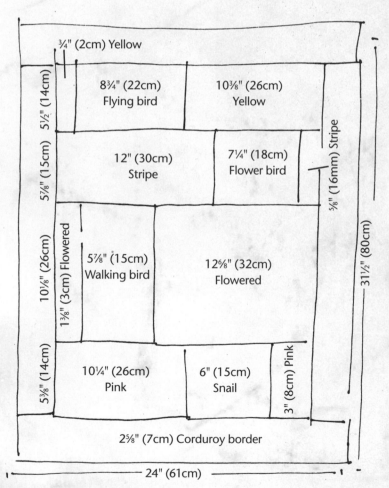

¾" (2cm) Yellow

5½" (14cm)

5⅞" (15cm)

8¾" (22cm) Flying bird

10⅜" (26cm) Yellow

12" (30cm) Stripe

7¼" (18cm) Flower bird

⅝" (16mm) Stripe

10⅛" (26cm)

1⅜" (3cm) Flowered

5⅞" (15cm) Walking bird

12⅝" (32cm) Flowered

31½" (80cm)

5⅜" (14cm)

10¼" (26cm) Pink

6" (15cm) Snail

3" (8cm) Pink

2⅝" (7cm) Corduroy border

24" (61cm)

Denim Quilt Diagram These are finished measurements. Add ¼" (6mm) seam allowance.

Step 3 Using the patterns as your guide (see pages 138–139), begin embroidering a bird or snail with a full six strands of embroidery thread (see *Embroidery Techniques*, pages 136–137). Tie all the knots on the underside of your work. Use French knots for the tail and antennea ends, eyes and flower centers. Remove the piece from the hoop and begin embroidering the next bird on another section of the denim. Be careful to leave a generous border of fabric around each embellishment.

Step 4 Once you've embroidered all four designs, choose a fabric to pair with each denim piece. Follow the diagram to trim both the fabric and the denim to the appropriate sizes. Machine sew the selected fabric to either side of each denim piece to create four horizontal strips. Sew the bottom of one strip to the top of another until you've joined all four together to create your quilt top. Frame the finished top with a 2⅝" (7cm) corduroy border. Placing right sides together, lay the quilt top and curtain backing together. Place them over the flannel batting. Machine stitch around all four sides, trapping all three layers and leaving a 8" (20cm) opening to pull the finished quilt right side out. Insert your batting through the opening, making sure it fully stretches inside the fabric. Use straight pins to anchor all three thickness together. Hand sew the opening closed. Use a darning needle and a full strand of embroidery floss to make a stitch from the quilt top to the bottom and back up again each denim corner. Securely knot the thread before trimming the ends an inch from the knot.

When our neighbors installed energy efficient windows, they placed their original wooden window frames on the curb. We gratefully loaded them in our trunk, knowing they would make gorgeous cold frames. Maine has a terribly short growing season, and a well-functioning cold frame allows us to stretch the season and set outside seedlings early. Simply open the window during the day so sunlight and heat can warm the plants. When you close the frame at night, the seedlings are protected from dropping temperatures.

Window Sash Cold Frame

 ## What a Green Idea!

Start seeds indoors and transplant greens to the cold frame for an early crop. Plant vegetable and flower starts directly into prepared garden soil when the weather has warmed. You'll reap the benefits of this endeavor all summer long.

Find more seasonal ideas in *Living the Green Life* on pages 36–37.

Materials List

RECYCLED MATERIALS
Old window sash
Scrap wood 1" × 8" (3cm × 20cm)
Leftover paint

TOOLS & SUPPLIES
Saw
Sandpaper
1½" (4cm) screws
Drill
Paintbrush

OTHER MATERIALS
Two hinges

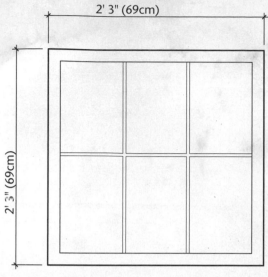

2' 3" (69cm)

2' 3" (69cm)

Diagram 1: Top View

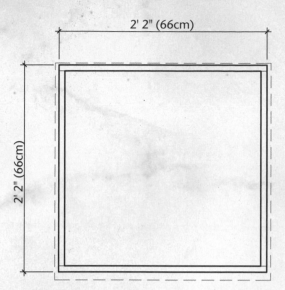

2' 2" (66cm)

2' 2" (66cm)

Diagram 2: Framing Plan

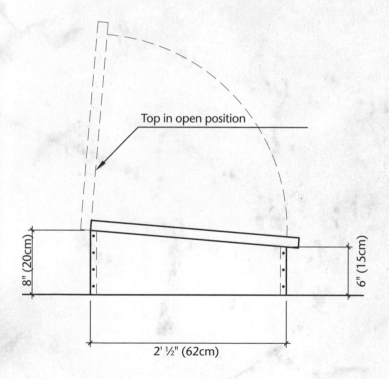

Top in open position

8" (20cm)

6" (15cm)

2' ½" (62cm)

Diagram 3: Side View

Step 1 Cut the boards of scrapwood into four lengths to match the dimensions of each side of your sash (see Diagram 1). The side boards are cut at an angle, 6" (15cm) deep in the front and 8" (20cm) in the back. Sand away rough edges.

Step 2 Pre-drill the holes so the screws don't split the ends of the wood. Screw together the corners using a screwdriver or drill. Evenly space three screws to join each of the front corners. Use four screws to join the high back corners (see Diagram 2).

Step 3 If desired, paint your box and allow it to dry completely before joining the window sash.

Step 4 To join the sash to the box, screw one side of the hinges to the top back of the box frame. Screw the other sides directly to the window sash. Be sure that your window easily opens and closes to allow airflow.

Tony DiPietro's lovely yard is a haven for the birds. His interest in building birdhouses began when his daughter brought home a handcrafted birdhouse from a local craft sale. Once a pair of swallows moved in and nested, Tony was hooked on the craft. He builds his custom bird homes out of reclaimed wood and embellishes his clever designs with salvaged tools and fixtures. To see more examples of his work, check out his website at www.birdhousesfrommaine.com.

Reclaimed Wood Birdhouse

Materials List

RECYCLED MATERIALS
Scrap wood (in this case, an old wooden crate)
Shovel handle
Ladle

TOOLS & SUPPLIES
Saw
Drill with hole saw bit
Hammer
Nails

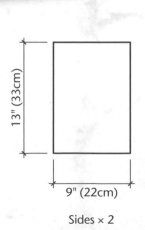

13" (33cm)

9" (22cm)

Sides × 2

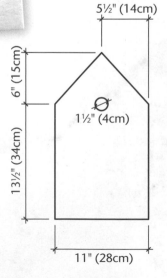

5½" (14cm)

6" (15cm)

1½" (4cm)

13½" (34cm)

11" (28cm)

Front & Back

Diagram 1: Cutting Diagram

34

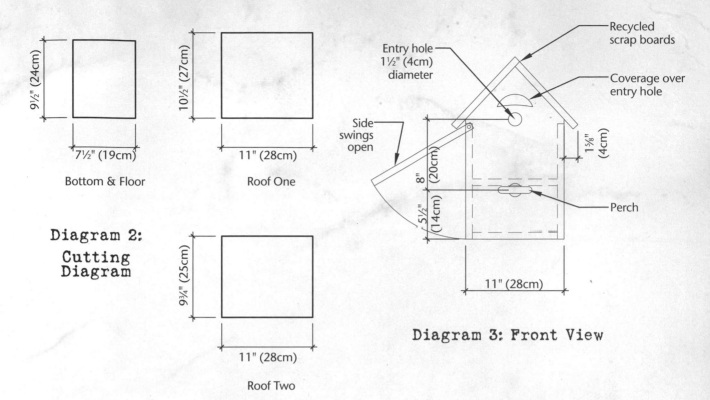

9½" (24cm)

7½" (19cm)

Bottom & Floor

10½" (27cm)

11" (28cm)

Roof One

Diagram 2: Cutting Diagram

9¾" (25cm)

11" (28cm)

Roof Two

Entry hole 1½" (4cm) diameter

Recycled scrap boards

Coverage over entry hole

Side swings open

8" (20cm)

5½" (14cm)

1⅝" (4cm)

Perch

11" (28cm)

Diagram 3: Front View

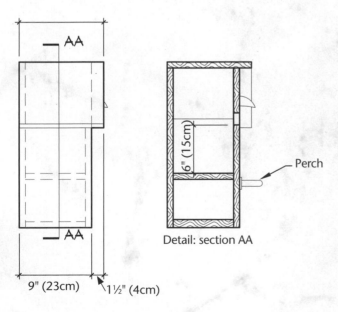

AA

AA

6" (15cm)

Perch

Detail: section AA

9" (23cm)

1½" (4cm)

Diagram 4: Side View

Step 1 First, select and cut an interesting board for the front of the house. Cut the rest of the pieces from the remaining wood (see Diagrams 1 and 2). Adjust the measurements as needed to work with your found materials.

Step 2 Use a hole saw attachment to drill a 1½" (4cm) hole in the front of the house. Make sure the hole will be located 4" to 5" (10cm to 13cm) above the floor for small birds like swallows or sparrows, or 6" to 7" (15cm to 18cm) for larger birds like bluebirds.

Step 3 Nail the remaining side piece to the top of the box using a nail on each side to allow it to pivot open for cleaning (see Diagram 3).

Step 4 Nail the remaining side piece to the top of the box using a nail on each side to allow it to pivot open for cleaning (see Diagram 4).

Step 5 Nail the roof to the top of your finished house.

Step 6 Add fun and decorative embellishments to customize your creation. Drill holes in a ladle and screw it over the opening. Drill a larger hold to insert the shovel handle perch under the opening.

Living the Green Life:
Ideas, Activities & Recipes

Eco Ideas

Celebrate Earth Day (April 22) all season long with these great ideas:

o Use biofriendly cleaners. Baking soda is just one of many biofriendly cleaners you might have on hand (see page 10 for ways to use baking soda). White vinegar is good for cleaning windows with crumpled newspapers. Use it in combination with baking soda to make a foaming toilet bowl cleaner. Olive oil takes fingerprints off of stainless-steel appliances. If you need to purchase other home cleaning solutions, look for less synthetic products that use biodegradable, nontoxic ingredients.

o Declutter your home. Goodwill and the Salvation Army gladly take unwanted clothes, bedding and smaller household goods. Post larger items online at Freecycle (www.freecycle.com). You might find something you need while you're on the site. Habitat for Humanity (www.habitat.org) accepts tools, paint, building materials, furniture and working appliances. Do anything you can to avoid adding your unwanted items to a landfill.

o Compost vegetable scraps, coffee grounds and eggshells. Either purchase a compost bin or simply create a fenced area. Collect scraps in a covered container in your kitchen and dump the contents into your compost. Rotate or shovel the contents regularly to aerate. Not only will you have rich soil for your garden, you'll reduce waste.

o Actively help keep parks and water clean of garbage by organizing and participating in a neighborhood or community cleanups. Donate the money from bottle redemption to an Earth-friendly charity.

Relax, Unwind & Unplug

The days are getting longer, so make the most of them with these springtime activities:

o Take a walk after dinner.

o Take a hike or walk on local nature trails, and keep your eye out for morel mushrooms, fiddleheads and returning birds.

o Make a green centerpiece. Sprout grass seeds in a real decorated eggshell.

o Help with a community garden near you; buy a share in a local organic farm.

Foods for the Season

Just when we feel like winter will never end, the first signs of spring appear, and we can look forward to fresh greens from the garden and the sweet taste of strawberries. If you're pressed for time, a dinner salad is the perfect solution. The quiche takes minutes to assemble but requires time to bake. Pizza is in and out of the oven in less than twenty minutes; there's really no reason to call for delivery.

HUMMUS

The perfect snack food, hummus is quick, easy and nutritious. This recipe makes a great deal more than the small packaged varieties at the grocery store. My high school-aged son makes this recipe on his own`. . . If only I could get him to clean the food processor!

3 cloves garlic
½ cup loose flat-leaf parsley, stems removed
2 16-ounce cans garbanzo beans, rinsed and drained
6 tablespoons tahini (sesame butter) (available in the ethnic aisle of most grocery stores)
Juice from one lemon
1 teaspoon salt

1. Place all the ingredients in the bowl of a food processor and cream until smooth. Scrape down the sides to make sure everything is well incorporated.
2. Serve immediately with pita triangles, carrots, celery and broccoli. Refrigerate leftovers in a tightly sealed container.

o o o o o o o o o o o o o o o o o o o

CRABMEAT LEEK QUICHE

Spring in Maine brings fabulous deals on shrimp and crabmeat. If you're landlocked or not a seafood fan, please give this recipe a second look. I use it as a base for different vegetable combinations all year long. Simply replace the crab and leek with your favorites. A quick dinner solution, consider making two different pies at the same time. You'll have delicious leftovers for breakfast.

4–6 eggs
1 cup 1% milk
salt, pepper and nutmeg
1 leek, sliced thinly
6 ounces crabmeat
1 cup shredded swiss cheese
1 pie crust

1. Preheat the oven to 350°F.
2. Beat eggs, milk, salt, pepper and nutmeg together. Add leek, crabmeat and cheese. Pour into prepared crust.
3. Bake 40–50 minutes until pie is completely set and knife comes out clean.

o o o o o o o o o o o o o o o o o o

SPINACH MUSHROOM PIZZA

I never get tired of pizza. You can easily adapt your veggies to whatever is in season. Pairing mozzarella with ricotta, feta or Neufchatel adds elegance to your pie. I love to make pizza when it's still cool outside. The house benefits from the pre-heated oven, and the hot pie warms your belly. Stock dough and cheese in your freezer so you won't be tempted to drive to satisfy your pizza cravings

1 tablespoon butter
1 small onion
Mushrooms, sliced
Spinach, rinsed and stems removed
Prepared pizza dough (If necessary, leave it on the counter to warm to room temperature.)
Cornmeal
2 cloves garlic, minced
2 tablespoons olive oil
Purchased pizza sauce
2 cups mozzarella, provolone and asiago shredded cheese mixture

1. Place a pizza stone in the center of the oven, then preheat to 450°F.
2. Melt the butter in a skillet. Sauté the onion until translucent. Add the mushrooms, and lightly sauté. Add the spinach and garlic. Stir to combine. Remove from heat when wilted.
3. Gently pull the pizza dough to stretch it into a round shape. Spread a thin layer of cornmeal on your pizza stone or baking sheet. Lay the shaped dough over the cornmeal.
4. Brush olive oil over the surface of the dough. Spread ¼ cup of the sauce over the center of the dough.
5. Transfer the onion, mushroom, spinach and garlic combination over the sauce. Sprinkle with a generous amount of cheese.
6. Place in the oven and bake for 10 minutes or until cheese bubbles and the crust has browned.

SPRING GREENS SALAD WITH MARK AND JAN'S HOMEMADE DRESSING

Celebrate the first greens of the summer with a delicious dinner salad. The addition of eggs, leftover chicken or sliced steak off the grill adds protein. Dried cranberries, nuts and cheese lend sweetness, crunch and creaminess. Our favorite homemade dressing makes a perfect complement.

Fresh greens, rinsed and torn
Spring peas, peeled
Chicken, steak or hard-boiled eggs, cut into slices
Dried cranberries
Walnuts
Grated or crumbled cheese

Mark and Jan's Dressing
1 teaspoon each of the following:
   salt
   onion powder
   dry mustard
   paprika
   celery salt
2 tablespoons sugar
½ cup vinegar
1 cup oil

1. Divide the greens among your plates.
2. Arrange the peas and the chicken, steak or eggs over the greens. Sprinkle cranberries, walnuts and cheese over the salad.
3. Pour all the ingredients for the dressing into a well-cleaned dressing bottle. Shake well and pour the desired amount on salad. Store leftover dressing in the refrigerator.

o o o o o o o o o o o o o o o o o o

STRAWBERRIES WITH BALSAMIC VINEGAR

It's difficult to imagine an improvement on fresh strawberries, but the sweetness, spice and tang of this marinade does just that. Your company will be amazed.

6 ounces fresh strawberries, stems removed, cut in half
2 tablespoons balsamic vinegar
¼ cup white sugar
Freshly ground black pepper
Vanilla ice cream

1. Place strawberries in a bowl. Pour the vinegar and sugar over the berries. Cover and let them marinade at room temperature for at least an hour.
2. Just before serving, grind a scant dusting of black pepper over the mixture. Serve the berries and their sauce over vanilla ice cream.

Chapter 2
summer

Fun, fun in the summer sun! Take advantage of the beautiful weather to throw a crochet T-shirt Frisbee and hang your laundry out to dry with the help of a clothespin owl. When you're out exploring, be on the lookout for interesting pieces of driftwood, smooth, flat pebbles and shells. This chapter features some simple jewelry- and tile-making techniques to help transform these natural treasures into stunning mobiles and classic stone coasters.

One of my favorite parts of summer is buying local produce at the farmers market in the center of town on Tuesdays and Fridays. Bringing your own bag has become more commonplace, but bringing a bag that's made from used plastic bags or chip bags is still a novelty. If you're a knitter, check out my directions for making plarn (plastic yarn), or if machine stitching is more your bag, get out your iron to fuse layers of plastic together into a colorful waterproof fabric. You can also fold and link potato chip bags sections together to make a one-of-a-kind handbag.

Summer is the perfect time to get planting; you'll attract hummingbirds, bees and butterflies into your garden, and also reap the benefits of fresh herbs and vegetables. Every gardener will appreciate a fabulous outdoor potting bench made with an old door and salvaged sink for keeping the mess and supplies in one place. Now's the time to get your houseplants into the sun and warmth and upgrade them into larger, newly crafted mosaic pots. You might also consider the benefits of shading your home with a whimsical ladder trellis that blooms plastic-lid flowers. It's sturdy enough to support a heavy vine and adds color all year long.

What a Green Idea!

Catch a wave! Go swimming in a wading pool, pond, lake or ocean, and splash into summer.

Find more summertime activities in *Living the Green Life* on pages 68–69.

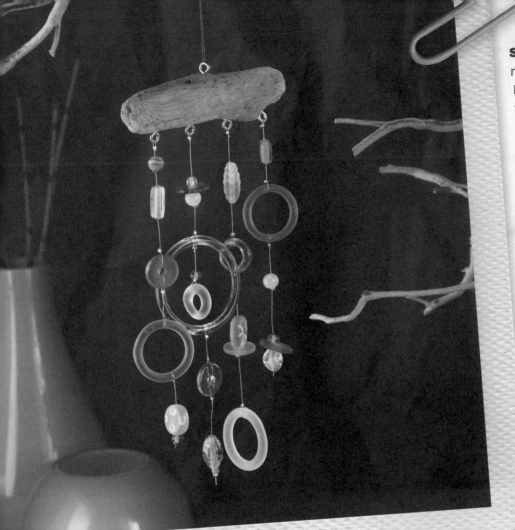

Summertime at the beach is what makes living through long, cold Maine winters worthwhile. Low tide is the best time for finding sea glass and shells, but driftwood usually settles along the high tide line, making it easy to collect any time of day. We're always toting treasures home from the beach in sandy buckets. These mobiles are the perfect way to transform these finds into stunning wind chimes. Eye screws are easily pushed into the underside of the wood. Sections of jewelry-stringing wire are crimped to each eye screw to securely attach beads and glass.

Materials List

RECYCLED MATERIALS
5" (13cm) driftwood branch

OTHER MATERIALS
Small eye hooks
Assorted glass beads
Connect glass rings (Plaid)
Crimp beads

TOOLS & SUPPLIES
Awl or nail punch
Flush cutters
7 strand .015" (.4mm) stringing
  wire (Beadalon)
Pliers

RESOURCES
Finished Length: 9½" (24cm)

Driftwood & Glass Mobile

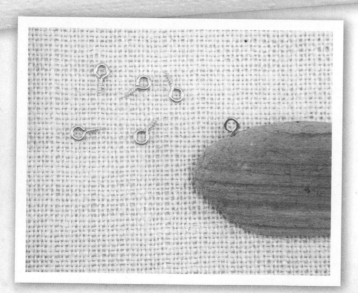

Step 1 Use an awl to punch four evenly spaced holes 1" (3cm) apart in the underside of your driftwood. Twist eye hooks into the wood until the eye sits right on top of the wood. Next, cut the stringing wire into 3" to 5" (8cm to 13cm) lengths.

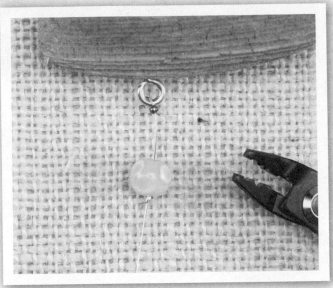

Step 2 Lay four rows of beads and glass rings on your work surface. Distribute the colors, sizes and finishes between the rows, while also considering how the beads and glass rings will interact in the wind. String a crimp bead onto your first section of wire. Then loop the wire end through the first eye hook. Next, string it back down through the crimp bead. Pull the wire loop tight and use your pliers to squeeze the bead flat.

Step 3 String the first section of your beading sequence onto the wire. To hold a bead in a specific position, thread a crimp bead under it and squeeze the crimp flat with your pliers. The flattened metal should hold the bead in place. If the glass bead has a large opening, you may need to add a small bead before the crimp to prevent it from getting swallowed in the large opening.

Step 4 To attach a glass ring to the end of a stringing wire, first string a crimp bead onto the wire. Then loop the wire around the ring and string the wire end back up through the crimp. Use pliers to flatten the crimp bead. Repeat the process to add a new wire below the ring.

Step 5 Finish each strand by adding a small bead followed by a crimp to the end of the stringing wire. Trim the wire end.

This project might be one of my favorite craft discoveries. I loved the simple layering of plastic bags and how the colors and graphic lettering instantly fused together with iron heat. Like magic, the fused pieces cut easily and feed effortlessly through a sewing machine. This allows you to sew different colored sections into a large tote bag. The sturdy handles are recycled tie-down webbing straps. The fused plastic is versatile and waterproof, making it a great material for other projects like book covers, bibs and placemats.

Fused Plastic Tote

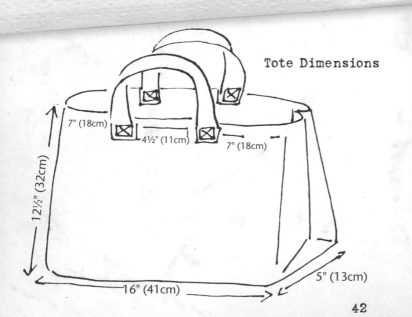

Tote Dimensions

7" (18cm)
4½" (11cm)
7" (18cm)
12½" (32cm)
16" (41cm)
5" (13cm)

Materials List

RECYCLED MATERIALS
Assorted plastic bags
2" × 18" (5cm × 46cm) sections of 1¼" (3cm) wide webbing (from tie-down straps)

TOOLS & SUPPLIES
Scissors
Iron and ironing board
Parchment paper
Rotary cutter, clear ruler and self-healing mat
Sewing machine

RESOURCES
Finished size: See *Tote Dimensions* illustration, left.

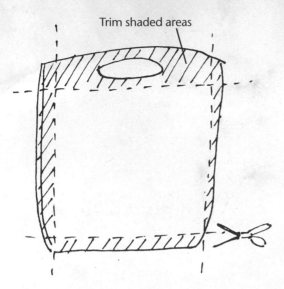

Trim shaded areas

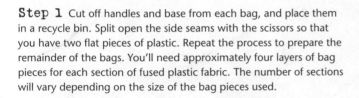

Step 1 Cut off handles and base from each bag, and place them in a recycle bin. Split open the side seams with the scissors so that you have two flat pieces of plastic. Repeat the process to prepare the remainder of the bags. You'll need approximately four layers of bag pieces for each section of fused plastic fabric. The number of sections will vary depending on the size of the bag pieces used.

Step 2 Set up the ironing board in a well-ventilated area. Place a sheet of parchment paper over your ironing board. Stack four bag sections over the parchment. I found that two pieces of the brightly colored heavyweight bags are best layered over two plain or clear lighter-weight bag sections. If you're using all lightweight plastic bags, you can increase the number of bags in each layer to make a stronger fabric. Place a second piece of parchment over the bags. You don't have to use solid sheets of plastic. You can collage the top two layers together in sections.

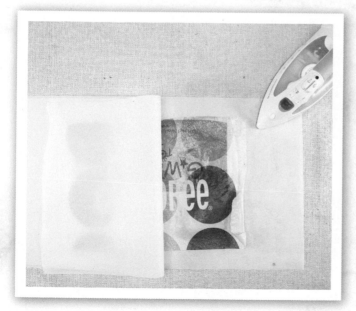

Step 3 Begin ironing over the top parchment paper. I used medium-high heat. You'll need to experiment to see what works best for you. Be careful that your iron doesn't come into direct contact with the plastic. It's important to keep the iron circulating; don't hold it over one area. You're trying to get even heating and melting and avoid any trapped air bubbles. Flip the whole stack over so that the top parchment is on the bottom and the bottom parchment is on the top. Repeat the ironing process. Lift up the corners of the paper to check the fusing process. I find the edges often need a second ironing. If it appears to be slightly shrunk and evenly fused, carefully remove it and let it cool. Repeat the process to make eight more pieces of fused plastic fabric, for a total of nine.

MORE STEPS

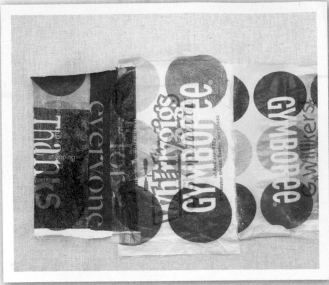

Step 4 Place a fused piece on a cutting board and start trimming the side edges of each piece using a rotary cutter and ruler.

Step 5 Machine stitch the side edges of three pieces together to make a strip. Overlap the edges and place them right side up in your machine. Use a long and tight zigzag stitch and seam down the middle of the cut edge so the stitch spans from one bag to the other. Repeat the process to make two more strips.

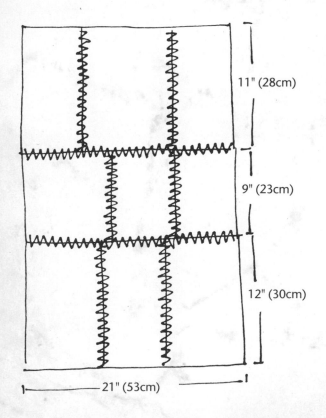

11" (28cm)

9" (23cm)

12" (30cm)

21" (53cm)

Step 6 Sew three strips together. Place each sewn strip on your cutting mat and use the ruler and rotary cutter to trim the top and bottom edges. Position your largest strips at the top and bottom; they'll become the front and back of your tote. Place the smallest piece in the middle; it'll become the base of your tote. Working with two strips at a time, stitch the bottom of one to the top of the other. You'll now have a single piece of fused fabric, the exact size isn't important. Use the dimensions in the illustration as a guide.

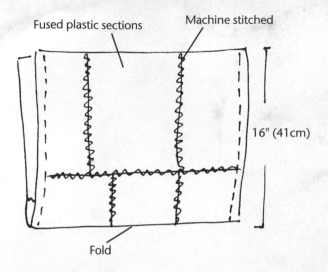

Fused plastic sections   Machine stitched

16" (41cm)

Fold

Step 7 Fold the fabric in half, right sides together, then seam the edges. Reinforce the side seams with a second zigzag stitch along the cut edge.

Step 8 Pull out the corners and flatten. Then sew a diagonal 5" (13cm) seam to create a triangle with the corner of the bag, making the top point. This will flatten the base of your bag.

Step 9 Turn over 1" (3cm) of the top edge, and machine stitch two straight seams to hold it in place. Cut and sear the web strap lengths with a match. Machine stitch them to the top front and back of the tote, approximately 7" (18cm) from the side seams. For added strength, stitch a box with a center **X** where the straps are attached to the bag.

Your grandma knew that hanging clothes out to dry in the sun was a good idea. It's time that we take a step back from technology and reap the natural benefits of solar- and wind-powered laundry drying. This clever owl clothespin holder will make the ritual more enjoyable. He's quickly made out of a T-shirt. The decorative fabric patches are ironed directly onto the T-shirt with the help of heat and bond interfacing. You'll need to break out the sewing needle only to affix the button eyes and beak to the owl's face.

Owl Clothespin Holder

What a Green Idea!

Hang clothes out to dry when weather permits, and use a drying rack indoors when the weather doesn't. To make your own drying rack, see the *Retractable Drying Rack* on pages 124–125.

Find more seasonal ideas in *Living the Green Life* on pages 68–69.

Materials List

RECYCLED MATERIALS
T-shirt
Fabric scraps, four different colors: green (for the feet), rust and brown (for the eye circles) and aqua (for the breast)
Two large round buttons (for the eyes)
Triangle button (for the beak)
Wooden or plastic hanger

TOOLS & SUPPLIES
Scissors
Iron and ironing board
Sewing machine
Sewing needle

OTHER MATERIALS
Interfacing
Thread

RESOURCES
Patterns: page 139
Finished size: 15" × 12½" (38cm × 32cm)

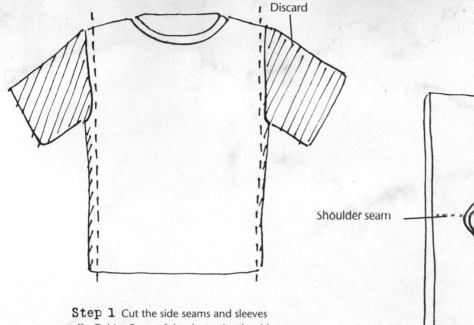

Discard

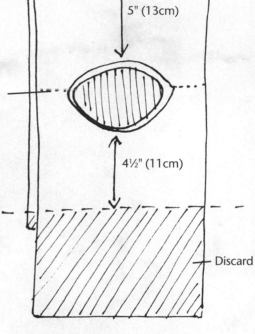

5" (13cm)

Shoulder seam

4½" (11cm)

Discard

Step 1 Cut the side seams and sleeves off a T-shirt. Be careful to leave the shoulder seams intact.

Opening for hanger

Neck opening

Step 2 Unfold the shirt and refold it, positioning the neck opening in the center front. It will become the opening for the clothespins. Leave 5" (13cm) above the top of the neck opening for the beak and eyes before folding the back of the shirt under the front. Trim both layers of the shirt 4½" (11cm) below the neck opening.

Step 3 Fold both thicknesses of the shirt in half lengthwise and shape the edges to resemble an owl. Cut a small slit opening for the hanger.

MORE STEPS

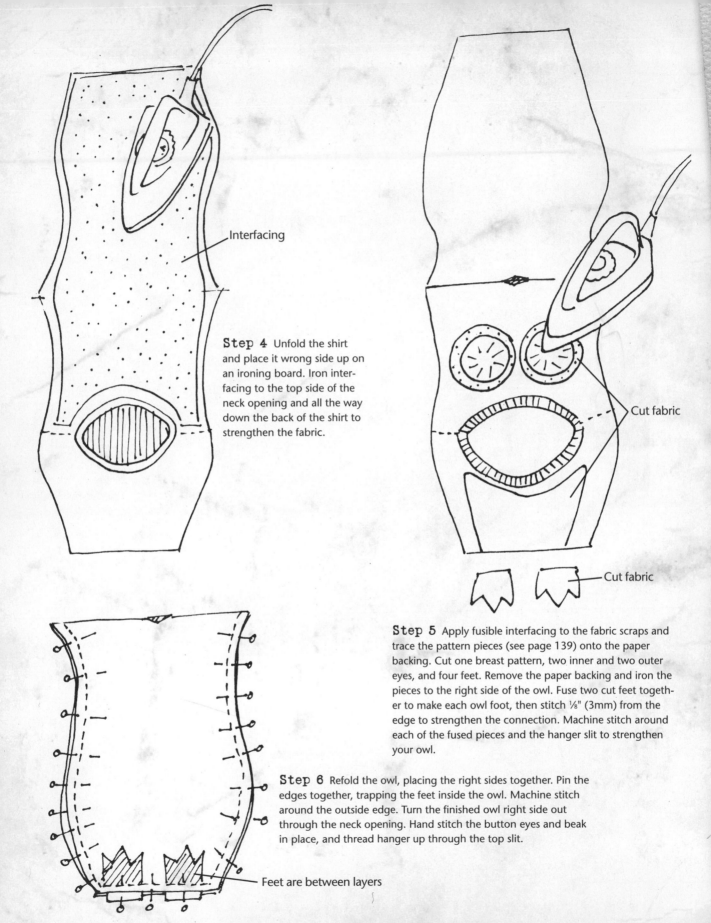

Interfacing

Step 4 Unfold the shirt and place it wrong side up on an ironing board. Iron interfacing to the top side of the neck opening and all the way down the back of the shirt to strengthen the fabric.

Cut fabric

Cut fabric

Step 5 Apply fusible interfacing to the fabric scraps and trace the pattern pieces (see page 139) onto the paper backing. Cut one breast pattern, two inner and two outer eyes, and four feet. Remove the paper backing and iron the pieces to the right side of the owl. Fuse two cut feet together to make each owl foot, then stitch ⅛" (3mm) from the edge to strengthen the connection. Machine stitch around each of the fused pieces and the hanger slit to strengthen your owl.

Step 6 Refold the owl, placing the right sides together. Pin the edges together, trapping the feet inside the owl. Machine stitch around the outside edge. Turn the finished owl right side out through the neck opening. Hand stitch the button eyes and beak in place, and thread hanger up through the top slit.

Feet are between layers

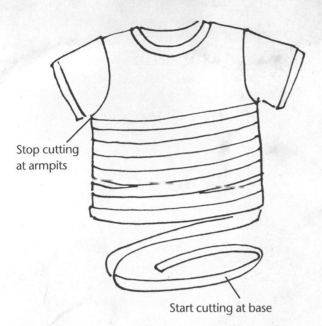

Stop cutting at armpits

Start cutting at base

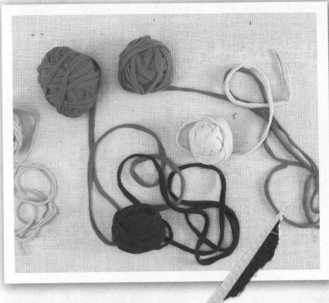

Step 1 To make the T-shirt yarn, cut the bottom hem off a T-shirt and discard. Then begin cutting a 1"-wide (3cm) continuous strip off the bottom of the shirt, working your way around the back of the shirt. Keep the scissors positioned an inch from the bottom edge and spiral your way up the shirt, ending at the armpits.

Step 2 Pull the strip taut as you roll it in a ball. This will cause the edges to curl in and make a tubular ... Repeat the process with the remaining T-shirts so that you have an assortment of colored yarns ready for crocheting.

Step 3 Use the following pattern to crochet the Frisbee (see Crochet Techniques, pages 134-135)

a.) Starting with light green, chain 3, connect it into a circle, then chain 1.

b.) Row 1: Single crochet 8 stitches.

c.) Row 2: Make 2 single crochet in each stitch for 16 stitches.

d.) Row 3: Change color to yellow and single crochet in each stitch for 16 stitches.

e.) Row 4: Single crochet in first stitch, make 2 single crochet in the next stitch, and repeat alternation to end of round for 28 stitches.

f.) Row 5: Change color to orange and single crochet in each stitch for 28 stitches.

g.) Row 6: Repeat Row 4 for 42 stitches.

h.) Row 7: Change color to pink and single crochet in each stitch for 42 stitches.

i.) Row 8: Change color to dark purple and repeat Row 4 for 64 stitches.

Step 4 To make the peace design, position the purple T-shirt yarn under the work. Push the crochet hook down through the top of the circle between the last two rounds, pink and purple. Hook the yarn and bring a loop back up to the top of the work. Repeat the process to continue making a straight line down the middle of the circle, bringing the hook down between each row. Cut the yarn end and weave it into your work. Join the yarn at the edge 3" (8cm) from the end of the vertical line where you'll begin making the diagonal line. Work your way up to the center of the Frisbee, then turn to make the second diagonal line. You'll be working your way back down the edge 3" (8cm) from the other side of the vertical line. Weave in the ends.

If you've ever folded a chain of gum wrappers, you've already mastered the key technique to making this unique purse. Foil chip bags are the perfect choice for building a tote: They have large, colorful surfaces, and they're both resilient and waterproof. To prepare the bags, eat the contents, clean away the salt and grease, and precut the bags into even-sized strips before folding. A handy credit card needle weaves fishing line through the strips to connect them together. This conversation starter is perfect accessory for the mom of a teenager, who has a perpetual supply of emptied food bags.

Snacker's Bag

Materials List

RECYCLED MATERIALS
Approximately forty mylar bags (chip, popcorn, pretzel, etc.)
Magazine or catalog pages

OTHER MATERIALS
Purse handles (Prym-Dritz Corp.)

TOOLS & SUPPLIES
Rotary cutter, clear ruler and self-healing mat
Craft knife or paper cutter

Scissors
Bone folder
Old credit card
Needle
Supplemax (Beadalon) or fishing line
1/8" (3mm) hole punch or awl
Stapler

RESOURCES
Finished size: 10" x 11" (25cm × 28cm) with 3½"-high (9cm) handles

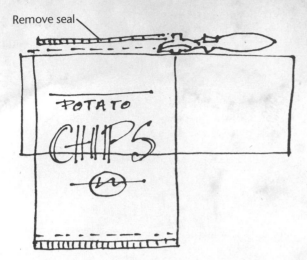

Remove seal

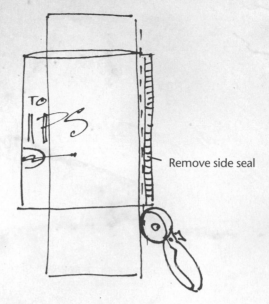

TO
||PS

Remove side seal

Step 1 Rinse, clean and dry all the bags. A large chip bag should yield seven to nine strips, depending on its dimensions. Individual-sized bags may only yield one to two strips. You'll need 324 strips to make this tote.

Working over a cutting mat, use a ruler as your guide to cut the top and bottom sealed edges off the bag with a rotary cutter.

Step 2 Unfold the bag and pull out the seam at the back of the bag. Refold the bag flat with the seam on the right edge. Use the ruler and rotary cutter to cut the seam off the side of the bag. Spread the bag open; you should be left with a single thickness of mylar bag.

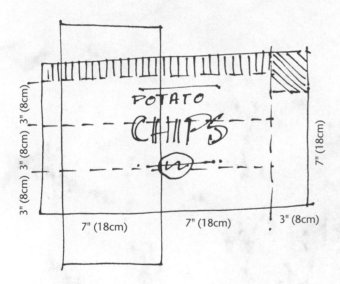

3" (8cm) 3" (8cm) 3" (8cm)

7" (18cm)

7" (18cm)   7" (18cm)   3" (8cm)

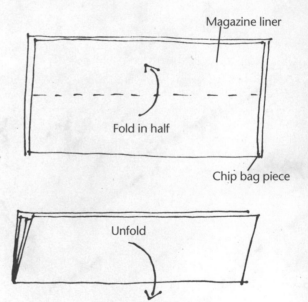

Magazine liner

Fold in half

Chip bag piece

Unfold

Step 3 Working over the mat, divide the bag into 7" (18cm) sections, then cut each section into 3" (8cm) widths. Get as many 3" × 7" (8cm × 18cm) pieces out of a bag as you can. Depending on the dimensions of the bag, you may get more pieces by cutting the bag a different way. Once you've cut all the bags, use a craft knife or paper cutter to cut an equal number of magazine paper liners in the same dimensions, 3" × 7" (8cm × 18cm).

Step 4 To fold the bag strips into links, follow the next four steps. First, place a mylar strip facedown on your work surface and spread a paper liner over the strip. From here on, fold both pieces together as if they are a single piece. Fold the strip in half lengthwise, crease the fold with your fingernail (or bone folder) and then unfold.

MORE STEPS

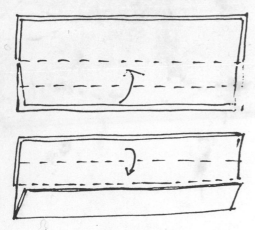

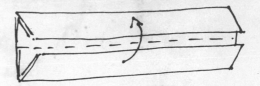

Step 6 Refold the piece in half lengthwise along the original fold line, trapping the folded top and bottom edges in the middle.

Step 5 Bring the bottom edge up to the center fold line and crease the fold. Bring the top edge down to the center fold line and crease the fold.

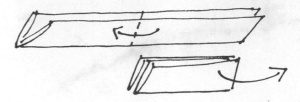

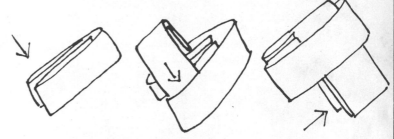

Step 7 Fold the piece in half widthwise, crease the fold and then unfold.

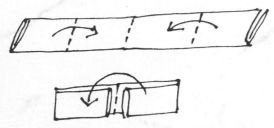

Step 8 Fold the left and right outside edges into the center fold line and crease the folds. Fold the piece in half along the fold line created in Step 7, trapping the ends inside the fold—you have now completed a prong. Get busy and repeat this sequence to transform 320 mylar strips/paper liners into links.

Step 9 To connect the links into chains, hold your first link in your hand with the folded crease at the top and the two prongs at the bottom. Connect a second link to the first by feeding each leg inside the prong ends of the first link. Slide the link until it's firmly locked in place.

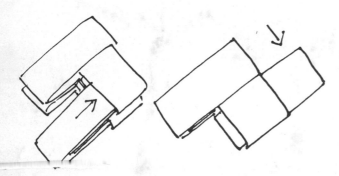

Step 10 Connect a third link to the chain, feeding its prongs up through the ends of second link. Slide it in place and then push a fourth link down through the prong ends of the third link. Continue adding links to the chain until you have a total of 39 links to create a long enough loop to span the front and back of your tote. You'll need a total of eight chains this length to stack together to make the tote tall enough.

Step 11 Once you've finished the chains, you'll need to connect each one into a loop. To do this, bring the first and last links together and connect them with a fortieth link. You'll need to push the prongs of the new link down through the top link end, and then open its ends and feed them around through the center of the bottom link ends. You'll know you've done it right if the link fits into the established pattern. Repeat the process to connect each of the remaining seven chains into 40-link loops.

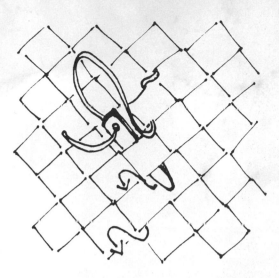

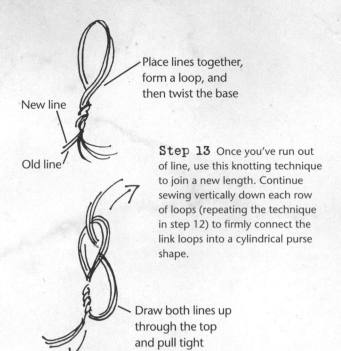

Place lines together, form a loop, and then twist the base

New line

Old line

Step 13 Once you've run out of line, use this knotting technique to join a new length. Continue sewing vertically down each row of loops (repeating the technique in step 12) to firmly connect the link loops into a cylindrical purse shape.

Draw both lines up through the top and pull tight

Slip needle inside a fold to begin stitching up next row.

Step 12 Stack one loop over another so that the zigzags nestle together. Use scissors to cut a rounded flat needle shape out of an old credit card. Punch a hole in the top end, or use an awl to create an opening. Thread the needle with a double thickness of Supplemax or fishing line. Use the needle to stitch the top of one loop to the bottom of the other (see illustration). Make sure the Supplemax or fishing line connects the pieces at the corners and is not visible across the chip bag links.

Step 14 Flatten the bottom of the connected cylindrical loops to bring the base of the tote together. With the exclusion of the two outer links, the zigzag chain teeth should fit together. Use a generous amount of line to sew them in place. Push the end teeth down inside the corners of the tote and, if possible, stitch them in place.

Step 15 To connect the handles, fold four links as shown in steps 1-5 and then fold them in half lengthwise again. Use a link to connect the handle to the inside top of the purse. Thread the link through the hole in the purse handle, and then pull the length halfway through. Thread the back strip end down through a link one row down from the top edge of the tote. Bring the other end down in front, and then staple them together directly under the link. Thread the joined ends down through the next link. Then fold the edges up under the last link for a clean finish. Repeat the process to attach the other end of the handle and the second handle to the other side of the bag.

Who knew that you could knit with plastic bags? It's actually an easy and amazing process. Plastic shopping bags are effortlessly folded and cut into loops that hook together to make a length of colored plarn (plastic yarn). Like a yarn dyer, you can create your own color combinations as you loop the pieces of plastic together. There are no fancy stitches or techniques, just regular knitting with a squeaky yarn. The resulting knitted fabric is durable, water-resistant and elastic, allowing the bag to stretch and accommodate large items.

Knitted Plarn Tote

Materials List

RECYCLED MATERIALS
Assorted lightweight plastic bags

TOOLS & SUPPLIES
Scissors
H crochet hook
15mm circular needles

RESOURCES
Knitting Techniques: pages 130–133
Finished size: 11" × 4" (28cm × 10cm) at base
19" × 4" (48cm × 10cm) with handle

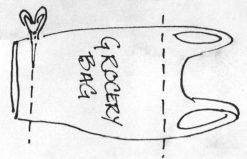

Step 1 Lay a bag flat on your work surface. Use scissors to cut off the top and bottom of the bag.

Step 2 Fold the bag in half.

Step 3 Fold it in half two more times so that you have a compact length.

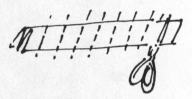

Step 4 Cut the length into 1" (3cm) sections.

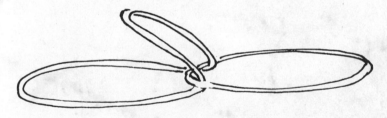

Step 5 Unfold two bag sections into loops. To connect the loops, thread the end of one loop into the top of the other.

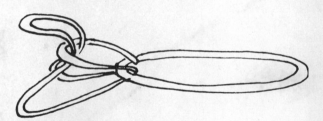

Step 6 Pull the end of the second loop back through itself to link it to the first loop.

Step 7 Use gentle pressure to pull the linked loop straight and flatten the connection section Repeat the process to link a third loop to the end of the second loop. Continue adding loops to create plastic yarn.

MORE STEPS

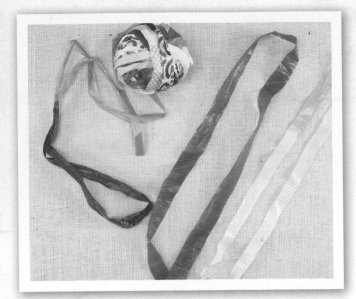

Step 8 Think of joining plastic loops as a way of custom dying your yarn. If you continue with one type of bag for a long time, it will create a strong stripe in the finished tote. If you constantly switch, you'll have a more variegated pattern. I did a little of both, switching bag varieties every two to three loops for the yarn used at the tote base, and then repeating six or more loops of the same color for the top of the tote to make broader stripes. You can roll up as much or as little plastic yarn as you wish before casting on. A generous 12" (30cm) ball should give you enough plastic yarn to make the tote, but if it doesn't, it's easy to loop on some more.

Step 9 Use the following pattern to knit the tote (see *Knitting Techniques*, pages 130–133):

a.) Cast on 30 stitches. Garter stitch 14 rows.

b.) Place a marker and turn the needle to purl 8 stitches from the side of the knitted section, purl 30 stitches across the cast on edge and purl 8 stitches from the remaining side, for a total of 76 stitches.

c.) Knit in the round until the piece measures 10" (25cm) or desired length.

d.) Knit 1, purl 1 for the next 6 stitches. Place marker and purl 18. Place marker and knit 1, purl 1 for the next 20 stitches. Place marker and purl 18, knit 1, purl 1 for 12 stitches.

e.) Rib the 20 stitches of the handle sections and knit the 18 stitches between the marker in the front and back of the purse.

f.) Rib the 20 stitches of the handle sections and pearl the 18 stitches front and back between markers.

g.) Rib the handle sections and bind off the 18 stitches front and back sections. Remove markers.

h.) Work each handle individually. Knit 2 together, rib 14, knit 2 together, 16 stitches.

i.) Rib 4 rows, decrease at either edge.

j.) Continue until you have 8 stitches left. Knit four rows. Use the plastic yarn to sew the 8 remaining stitches from each side of the handle together.

k.) Use a crochet hook to weave the plastic yarn end into the handle.

Chipped China Mosaic Pot

Now there's a reason to be happy when you break a favorite plate, cup or bowl! The shards will be perfect for a mosaic project. You can transform any plain pot into a piece of art. Find the perfect plant for your beautiful new pot, and enjoy the beauty and benefits of greenery in your home all year long.

Materials List

RECYCLED MATERIALS
Broken china and glass pieces

OTHER MATERIALS
Ceramic pot
Glass butterflies

TOOLS & SUPPLIES
Old towel
Rubber mallet
Eye protection
Tile nippers
Waterproof sealer
Tile adhesive (Plaid)
Plastic spoon and knife
Sanded grout
Sponge and bucket

Step 1 To prepare the glass and china, place the big pieces under a towel and break them with a mallet. Wearing eye protection, use tile nippers to control break any remaining large pieces.

Step 2 Prepare the pot by applying waterproofing to the interior, and let it dry. Apply a layer of adhesive to one side of the pot, leaving the rim and base uncovered. Press china and glass pieces and glass butterflies into the adhesive, they need to be firmly anchored. Repeat the process to apply adhesive to another section of the pot. Place them as close as possible, and try to distribute colors and varieties around the pot. Let the adhesive dry according to manufacturer's directions.

Step 3 Spoon grout over the adhesive, working it in between the china pieces. Once you've encircled the pot, move over a bucket of water and use a sponge to wipe the excess grout off the china and glass. Make sure the rim and base of the pot stay clean. Let the grout dry for 24 hours. Then scrub any remaining grout off the ceramic and glass.

When I first saw a handbag made out of bike inner tubes, I was intrigued. I wondered how easily the rubber could run through a sewing machine. I discovered that a single layer paired with heavyweight cotton fabric was much easier to sew than two layers of inner tube. The resulting zippered pouch has a heavy weight base, making it perfect for pens, pencils, crochet needles or makeup. If you don't have a spent inner tube in your garage, punctured inner tubes are readily available at any bike shop. Most shops recycle the tubes at a tire drop-off center and are more than happy to have you take some off their hands. A single inner tube makes several pouches and bags.

Zippered Inner Tube Pouches

Materials List

RECYCLED MATERIALS
Bike inner tube
Fabric scraps

OTHER MATERIALS
Zipper: 5" (13cm), 6" (15cm) or 9" (23cm)
Rubber tubing (Beadalon)
Wooden bead
Black upholstery thread

TOOLS & SUPPLIES
Scissors
Straight pins
Regular thread (match to fabric scrap)
Sewing machine (outfitted with a leather needle)

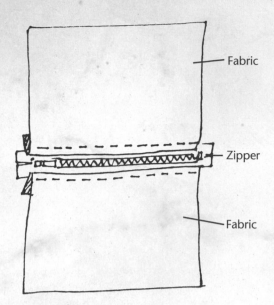

Fabric

Zipper

Fabric

Step 1 Cut around the inner tube to open it up into a flat piece of rubber. Cut two pieces of fabric and a single section of inner tube to the length of the zipper, and add an extra ½" (13 mm) of fabric along the top edge so you can fold it under to attach the zipper. The depth of your pouch is a matter of personal preference. The smaller pouch has a 5" (13cm) zipper and is 6" deep × 5½" wide (15cm × 14cm). A medium pouch has a 6" (15cm) zipper and is 9¼" deep × 6½" wide (23cm × 16cm). With two inner tube sections at the base, the wide pouch has a 9" (23cm) zipper and is 6½" deep × 9½" wide (16cm × 24cm). Make sure you also add a ¼" (6mm) seam allowance to the sides and base of each pouch.

Step 2 Lay the zipper out on your work surface. Working with the fabric right side up, fold under ½" (13mm) and pin the folded edge to one side of the zipper. Repeat on the other side. Thread your machine with the regular weight thread and replace your regular presser foot with a zipper foot. Stitch the fabric in place, removing the pins and adjusting the position of the zipper pull so it doesn't interfere with your seam. Repeat on the other side.

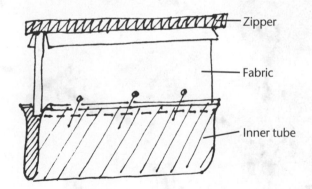

Zipper

Fabric

Inner tube

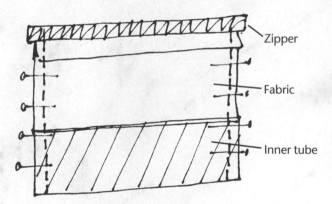

Zipper

Fabric

Inner tube

Step 3 Preparation: Refer to the owner's manual to familiarize yourself with the pressure settings of your sewing machine and adjust them to accommodate the most bulk possible. Switch the needle to a heavyweight leather needle, and thread both the bobbin and needle with heavyweight upholstery thread. Run a test scrap of fabric and inner tube through your machine. Make any necessary adjustments before sewing the pouch.

To begin, pin the bottom edge of the fabric to the top edge of the rubber, right sides together. Run the pinned fabric through your carefully prepared machine. Remove the pins as you sew. Repeat the process to attach the other side of the rubber to the second piece of fabric.

Step 4 Lay the pouch wrong side out on your work surface. Smooth it flat and pin the sides together, lining up the top edges of the rubber so that they make an even line around the base to the pouch. Fold the zipper into the pouch and pin the zipper tape ends together. Seam the sides closed, starting at the rubber bottom and working your way up to the zipper tapes. Trim away any loose threads. Slide the zipper open to pull the pouch right side out. Loop a 5" (13cm) section of rubber tubing through the zipper pull. String a wooden bead onto the ends and finish with an overhand knot.

Have you ever stopped to consider how many plastic milk, juice and soda bottle lids are discarded every day? They're bright, colorful, durable and waterproof, making them ideal for outdoor crafting. We discovered that short metal screws and an electric screwdriver make it easy to fasten them directly into cut plywood shapes. The resulting fanciful butterflies and flowers will bloom and flutter in your garden all year long. Two salvaged ladders are simply bolted together to make a sturdy trellis base. Once embellished with your bottle cap creations, all you need is a hardy vine to actively shade and cool your home all summer long.

Ladder Trellis

What a Green Idea!

Install a trellis to provide natural cooling near windows and doorways. Trellises work in two ways. First, they block the direct rays of the sun from entering the home. And second, they provide a framework for plants to grow. The plants help with shading, but they also help cool the air around them. As water evaporates, it releases energy that provides a cooling effect.

Find more seasonal ideas in *Living the Green Life* on pages 68–69.

Materials List

RECYCLED MATERIALS
Two salvaged wooden ladders
Large assortment of plastic lids
Painted scrap plywood (ours was around
    ½" (1cm) thick

TOOLS & SUPPLIES
Band saw or coping saw
Paintbrushes
Acrylic paint in a variety of colors
Waterproof sealer
¾" (19mm) wood screws
Drill
Two carriage bolts with washers and nuts
Hammer
Nails

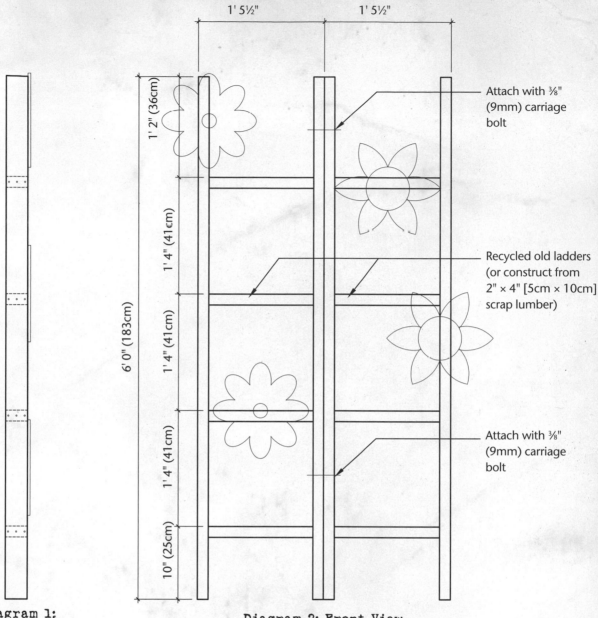

1' 5½"　　**1' 5½"**

1' 2" (36cm)

6' 0" (183cm)

1' 4" (41cm)

1' 4" (41cm)

1' 4" (41cm)

10" (25cm)

Attach with ⅜"
(9mm) carriage
bolt

Recycled old ladders
(or construct from
2" × 4" [5cm × 10cm]
scrap lumber)

Attach with ⅜"
(9mm) carriage
bolt

**Diagram 1:
Side View**

Diagram 2: Front View

Step 1 Trace an assortment of different sized simple flower, leaf and butterfly shapes onto plywood scraps. Use a band saw or coping saw to cut out the shapes. Round shapes are hard to cut, so square up your design if you want to simplify the cutting process. If desired, accent the shapes with acrylic paint. Brush waterproof sealer over the acrylic paint.

Step 2 Arrange the plastic lids, flat side down, over the flowers. I found tightly grouping the same colors in the flower centers to be a successful design solution. Also, repeating the same lid design on both of the butterfly

wings added simplicity and symmetry. Save green lids for the leaves. Once you've laid out all the lids on the flowers, you're ready to screw them in place.

Step 3 Select which flower you're going to work on first, and set the lids aside. Position a screw on the end of your drill and drive the center of the first lid in place. Continue attaching lids around the first one. Repeat the process with the remaining shapes.

Step 4 Drill a hole through both ladders where they will connect to each other, one at

the top and another at the bottom. Thread a carriage bolt through each hole and washer, and tightly screw the nut to the end of the bolt.

Step 5 Lay the attached ladders on the ground and begin arranging the flowers, leaves and butterflies over your trellis. Position the majority of the embellishment on the protruding vertical ladder posts. Use a hammer to nail them in place.

When our friends the Beatties moved into their new home this summer, this potting bench came with them. It's a fabulous piece of repurposed outdoor furniture, and it looks like it was custom-made for their new digs. Bart Beattie is the genius behind its creation. The sink caught his eye at a garage sale, and the potting bench was conceived and designed around it. The sink can be hooked directly to an outdoor hose, and a bucket under the drain captures wastewater for reuse. Bart's primary goal when building this project was to make his wife, Hannah, happy. Needless to say, he was successful. After all, who wouldn't love to have a charming outdoor work surface to repot plants and stage plantings in garden beds?

Planter's Potting Bench

 ## What a Green Idea!

Plant drought-resistant and native plants for landscaping to minimize or eliminate the need for irrigation around the house. These plants will also attract birds and beneficial insects.

Find more seasonal ideas in *Living the Green Life* on pages 68–69.

Materials List

RECYCLED MATERIALS
Wood door
Salvaged sink and boards
Wood shelf brackets

TOOLS & SUPPLIES
Saw
Hammer
Nails
Screws

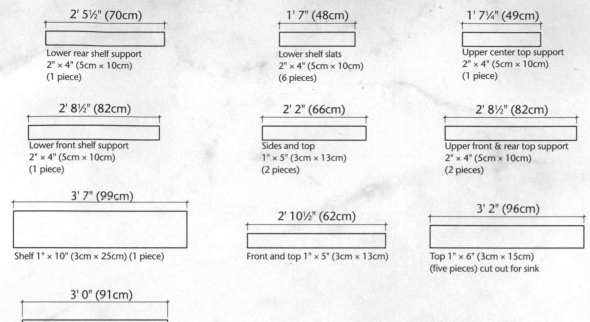

2' 5½" (70cm)

Lower rear shelf support
2" × 4" (5cm × 10cm)
(1 piece)

1' 7" (48cm)

Lower shelf slats
2" × 4" (5cm × 10cm)
(6 pieces)

1' 7¼" (49cm)

Upper center top support
2" × 4" (5cm × 10cm)
(1 piece)

2' 8½" (82cm)

Lower front shelf support
2" × 4" (5cm × 10cm)
(1 piece)

2' 2" (66cm)

Sides and top
1" × 5" (3cm × 13cm)
(2 pieces)

2' 8½" (82cm)

Upper front & rear top support
2" × 4" (5cm × 10cm)
(2 pieces)

3' 7" (99cm)

Shelf 1" × 10" (3cm × 25cm) (1 piece)

2' 10½" (62cm)

Front and top 1" × 5" (3cm × 13cm)

3' 2" (96cm)

Top 1" × 6" (3cm × 15cm)
(five pieces) cut out for sink

3' 0" (91cm)

Less 2" × 4" (5cm × 10cm) (4 pieces)
Rear door supports
2" × 4" (5cm × 10cm)
(6 pieces total)

Diagram 1: Cutting Diagram

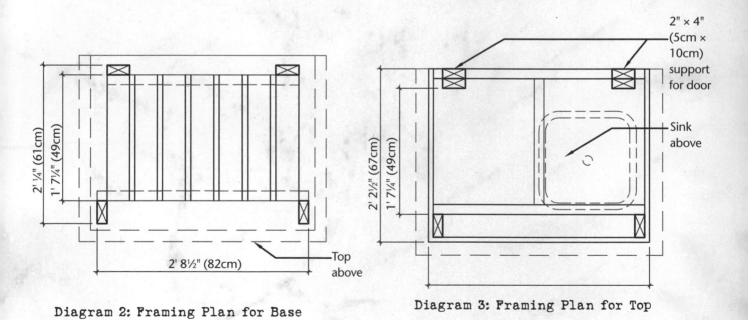

2' ¼" (61cm)
1' 7¼" (49cm)

2' 8½" (82cm)

Top above

Diagram 2: Framing Plan for Base

2" × 4" (5cm × 10cm) support for door

Sink above

2' 2½" (67cm)
1' 7¼" (49cm)

Diagram 3: Framing Plan for Top

MORE STEPS ➤

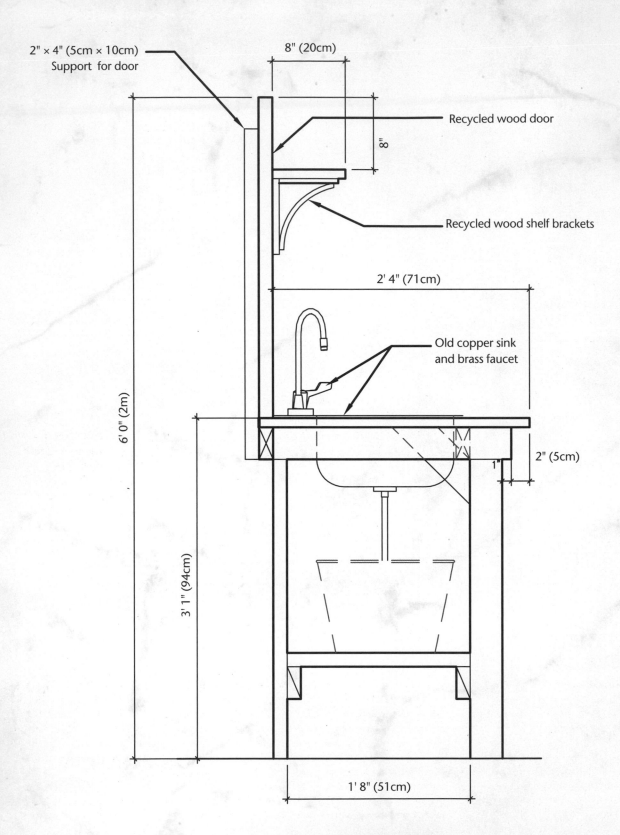

2" × 4" (5cm × 10cm)
Support for door

8" (20cm)

Recycled wood door

8"

Recycled wood shelf brackets

2' 4" (71cm)

Old copper sink
and brass faucet

6' 0" (2m)

2" (5cm)

1"

3' 1" (94cm)

1' 8" (51cm)

Diagram 4: Side View

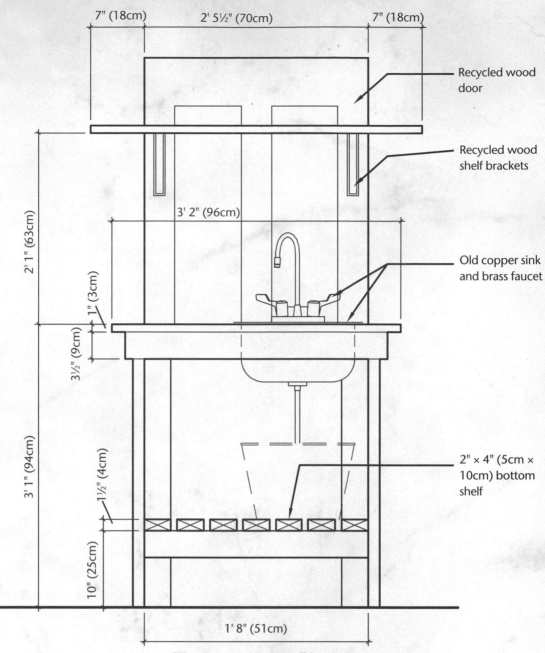

7" (18cm) 2' 5½" (70cm) 7" (18cm)

2' 1" (63cm)

3' 1" (94cm)

1" (3cm)

3½" (9cm)

1½" (4cm)

10" (25cm)

3' 2" (96cm)

1' 8" (51cm)

Recycled wood door

Recycled wood shelf brackets

Old copper sink and brass faucet

2" × 4" (5cm × 10cm) bottom shelf

Diagram 5: Front View

Step 1 Start with constructing the base. Cut 2" × 4" (5cm × 10cm) boards to lengths indicated in Diagram 1 (page 65) for the legs, braces, and shelves.

Step 2 Attach the horizontal supports to the back of the front legs and the front of the back legs, about 6" (15cm) above the ground. These will form the support for the boards that make up the bottom shelf.

Step 3 Attach the 2" × 4"s (5cm × 10cm) at the top of the table legs at the front, sides and back. Position the boards that will make up the top of the bench and determine where the hole for the sink will be located.

Step 4 Frame the opening with bracing to support the boards making up the bench top. Attach the boards for the top of the bench. Set the sink into the opening provided (see Diagram 3, page 65).

Step 5 Cut the wood door to 3' (91cm) in length. Attach the 2" X 4" (5cm X 10cm) rear door supports to the rear horizontal 2" X 4" (5cm X 10cm) support for the top. Screw through the wood door supports into the back of the door. Position the door on top of the bench top.

Step 6 Attach shelf support brackets as shown in Diagrams 4 and 5 (pages 66 and 67).

Step 7 Attach the shelf to the support brackets with screws.

Living the Green Life:
Ideas, Activities & Recipes

Eco Ideas

These ideas will help you get the most out of your summer, while impacting the environment the least:

o Buy your food at local farmers markets. This not only supports your local economy, it saves on fossil fuels; produce isn't flown and trucked across country. If you do shop at a retail store, look for locally grown and prepared merchandise. Whenever possible, select organically grown and raised meats and vegetables.

o Conserve drinking water by collecting and using rainwater to irrigate outdoor plants. Look for handy barrel collectors that connect to a downspout. Inside the house, don't let the tap run while waiting for cold drinking water—fill a pitcher and place it in your fridge. When waiting for warm tap water, collect the running water and use it to fill pet bowls, water plants and pre-soak dirty dishes. Run your dishwasher only when it's full. Avoid using or installing a garbage disposal. Install dams or displacement bags in your toilet tank to reduce the amount of water used with each flush. Try to keep your showers to five minutes.

o Consider the landscaping around your home. Trees and plantings should be arranged to provide natural screening against prevailing winter winds while maximizing solar exposure for winter passive heating. These same trees and plants can also provide maximum potential for the naturally cooling effects of prevailing summer breezes. Consult with a nursery or landscape architect if you need help.

o Garage sales are recycling outlets. Head out early with the newspaper listings, and keep your eye out for furniture that you can creatively revamp, toys and books that will appease your child's yearnings, and useful household goods and gadgets. I'm always surprised how many art and craft supplies I find.

Relax, Unwind & Unplug

These activities are perfect for long summer days, and they require no energy, except your own!

o Catch fireflies and let them go.

o Build forts out of driftwood or branches, or even miniature fairy houses with seed pods twigs, rocks and leaves.
o Pack a lunch or dinner and enjoy an outdoor concert or evening at a park.

Foods for the Season

Summer is a veritable paradise for anyone who loves to cook. Fresh herbs are steps away in the garden, and every week there's a colorful array of freshly picked vegetables and fruits at the farmers market. Grilling chicken and portabello mushrooms outside will keep the heat out of your home. If baking is a must, cook a batch of blueberry bread—it takes only ten minutes.

BLACK AND WHITE BEAN SALSA

This is our family's most popular dish. Whenever we serve it, everyone always asks for the recipe. Our friends Jim and Elizabeth Lewin introduced it to us it at a summer picnic ten years ago. It has the perfect blend of spices and vegetables. Once you've taken a bite, it's hard to stop piling more onto tortilla chips. Incredibly versatile and healthy, it can be made ahead and served with chips, on scrambled eggs or as a vegetarian entrée in warm tortillas.

3 tablespoons corn oil
2 cloves garlic
1¼ cup corn kernels
16-ounce can black beans rinsed and drained
16-ounce can great northern beans
1 each red, yellow and green bell peppers
1 medium red onion
2 tablespoons lime juice
1 teaspoon dried oregano
1 tablespoon chili powder
1½ teaspoon ground cumin
Salt and pepper
Fresh cilantro

1. Heat 1 tablespoon oil in a heavy skillet on high heat. Sauté garlic. Add corn and sauté until brown, about 3 minutes.
2. Combine the remaining 2 tablespoons of oil in a large bowl with all the other ingredients. Add the corn mixture to bowl. Season with salt, pepper and fresh cilantro.

GREEK PASTA SALAD WITH LIME DRESSING

This is the quintessential summer meal. I often have Jon grill extra chicken so that we have leftovers on hand to whip up this meal on a weekday. It makes a great main course and travels well on evening picnics to the beach. The only drawback: It doesn't last long with teenagers in the house.

16 ounces penne pasta
½ red onion
1 cucumber
1 pint of cherry tomatoes
Greek olives
Fresh basil, torn
Optional grilled chicken, cut into thin strips
6 ounces feta cheese, crumbled

Lime Dressing
Juice from one Lime
1/3 cup of extra virgin olive oil
¼ teaspoon white pepper
1 teaspoon of dried oregano
2 cloves of minced garlic

1. Cook the pasta in rapidly boiling water until it's al dente.
2. While the pasta is cooking, chop the onion and quarter and slice the cucumber. Then slice the cherry tomatoes and olives in half. Toss the vegetables and torn basil into a large mixing bowl. Add the grilled chicken strips and crumbled feta.
3. Drain the pasta and add to the bowl.
4. Combine the ingredients for the dressing in a bowl and whisk until well incorporated. Pour dressing over the pasta.
5. Stir the salad until the pasta, vegetables and chicken are well coated in dressing.

○ ○ ○ ○ ○ ○ ○ ○ ○ ○ ○ ○ ○ ○ ○ ○ ○ ○ ○

PORTABELLO SANDWICH

This hearty vegetarian dinner is the perfect alternative to hamburgers on the grill. The red wine vinegar marinade enhances the natural flavor of the mushroom. When topped with rich dressing, lettuce and tomato, I guarantee you won't miss the beef.

4 tablespoons olive oil
2 tablespoons red wine vinegar
2 teaspoons minced garlic
Salt and pepper

2 portabello mushroom caps
Whole wheat hamburger bun
Lettuce, torn
Tomato, sliced
Parmesan dressing

1. Whisk together the olive oil, red wine vinegar, garlic, salt and pepper. Pour over the mushroom caps (stem side up). Marinate for at least 10 minutes.
2. Preheat the grill or warm a skillet and cook the caps 6–8 minutes until browned and tender.
3. Serve the caps on buns, with lettuce, tomato and dressing, just like a traditional burger.

○ ○ ○ ○ ○ ○ ○ ○ ○ ○ ○ ○ ○ ○ ○ ○ ○ ○ ○

BLUEBERRY BREAD

This is an oldie but goodie that has withstood the test of time because it's quick, simple and delicious. In less than twenty minutes, you can have fresh blueberry bread on the table. Stick it in the oven while you scramble the eggs for breakfast or while the chicken grills for dinner. Last Fourth of July, the whole batch disappeared so quickly I made a second and had it on the table before everyone had finished eating.

2 cups flour
1 tablespoon baking powder
½ teaspoon salt
3 tablespoons sugar
½ cup butter
1 egg
¾ cup plus 1 tablespoon milk
1 cup of fresh or frozen blueberries

Topping
2 tablespoons sugar
½ teaspoon cinnamon

1. Preheat oven to 450°F.
2. Lightly butter baking sheet.
3. Mix the flour with baking powder, salt and sugar. Cut in the butter. Set aside.
4. Beat egg and milk together and pour into flour mixture. Mix just until moistened. Fold in blueberries.
5. Spread the sticky dough into a ½"-thick rectangle on a lightly buttered baking sheet. Sprinkle the top with sugar and cinnamon.
6. Bake for 10 minutes or until brown and a toothpick inserted in the center comes out clean.

Chapter 3
autumn

As the evenings turn cool and the days grow shorter, thoughts turn to the new school year. I've always loved gathering school supplies, but making your own from recycled materials is even more gratifying. Vinyl record album covers give used three-ring binders a facelift. Glossy magazine pages can be folded and glued into unique bowls and office trash baskets. Instead of tossing copy paper and cardboard food packaging in the recycling bin, consider cutting it and folding it to create handy matchbook-style notebooks and woven baskets. Sometimes used supplies themselves become the basis for making a new item, which is the case in the colored pencil watch strap.

If you're setting up a dorm room or apartment, this chapter features exciting ways to transform recyclables into home furnishings, lighting and accessories. Once you've unpacked your corrugated cardboard boxes, fold and slot them into a functional chair. Water bottles are cleverly melted, punched and tied into a hanging light fixture. Aluminum cans are easy to cut open and hammer around a mirror. Old rulers frame a homemade chalkboard to make a paper-free message center.

Compact discs are problematic to recycle, but I've come up with two clever ways to craft with this fabulous material. The first utilizes a single disc and punctuates it with computer keys to make a handy clock. The second slices a handful of CDs with scissors and reconnects them into a prismatic disco ball. Direct a light on it, turn up the music and host a party in your newly decorated digs.

What a Green Idea!
Grab a rake, make a pile and jump into autumn! Enjoy the fall foliage and the crisp, fresh air.

Find more autumn activities in *Living the Green Life* on pages 102–103.

Because of my husband's work, we have stacks of beautiful magazines filled with full-page architecture photographs. I was thrilled to find an ingenious way to repurpose the heavyweight pages. A series of simple folds compacts a single page into a long, sturdy strip. The strips are then tightly coiled and hot glued together. A protective coat of découpage medium preserves the finished bowl. This is a great group project; it's helpful to have lots of hands to fold pages.

Glossy Magazine Bowl

Project Note

The amount of color and type on the pages you fold will determine the look of your bowl. For example, wedding magazines create a predominantly white and pastel-colored bowl.

Materials List

RECYCLED MATERIALS
Five to six glossy full-color magazines

TOOLS & SUPPLIES
Glue gun and glue sticks
Wax paper
Mod Podge (Plaid) and glue brush

RESOURCES
Finished Size: 6½" × 10¾" (16cm × 27cm), with a 4½" (11cm) base

Step 1 Carefully rip a generous pile of pages from the magazines. Don't be concerned if you lose small amounts of the ripped edge; it will be concealed in the folds.

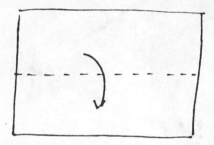

Step 2 Fold the page in half lengthwise, leaving the image you want on the outside. Crease the fold line with your fingernail.

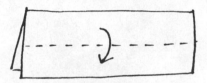

Step 3 Fold in half lengthwise again, crease.

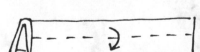

Step 4 Fold in half again, crease.

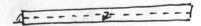

Step 5 Fold in half one final time.

Step 6 The folding transforms your ripped pages into narrow folded strips ready for coiling.

MORE STEPS

Step 7 Beginning in the center base of the bowl, tightly coil one end of your first strip, folded edge up. Apply a thin line of hot glue to the outside center of the coil. Wrap and press the remaining strip length into the glue. Add a second strip, folded side up, where the first strip ends. Continue applying a small line of glue to the center of the coiled paper, tightly wrapping new strips around the coil. The folded edges will become the outside of the bowl, and the rough edges will fall to the inside of the bowl.

Step 8 When the base is the desired size (this bowl is 4½" [11cm] in diameter), begin positioning the new strips 1/8" (3mm) up from the strip beneath it.

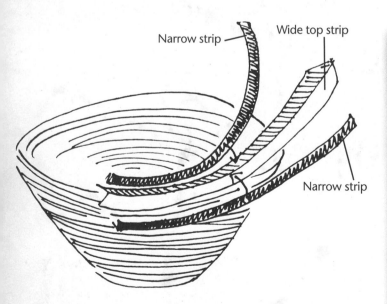

Narrow strip

Wide top strip

Narrow strip

Step 9 Continue adding strips, alternating colors and patterns until the bowl is 6½" (16cm) high, or the desired size. To finish the top edge, fold several strips in half lengthwise three times and glue them down so that the center fold covers the top edge. Fold another set of strips in half lengthwise five times and hot glue these narrow strips over the bottom edges of the wide top strip, placing them both on the inside and outside of the bowl. This will help integrate the top piece with the established pattern.

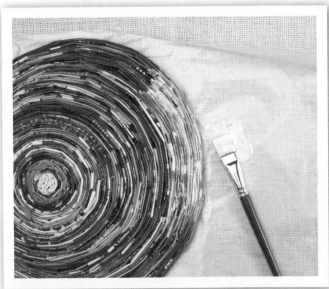

Step 10 Working over wax paper, apply a generous coat of Mod Podge to the outside and inside of the finished bowl.

CD Clock

Have you ever stopped to think of all the compact discs that become obsolete? Using one to create a perfectly, round lightweight clock face won't solve the problem, but it's a start. This white disc held a start-up program for my first Apple clamshell laptop. The function keys that mark the hours come from the very same computer. I wrote many articles and books on that beloved machine. The clock-works are salvaged from a promotional give-away. Combining these things made something new and functional out of something old. Take a fresh look at your used stuff, and you may discover that you have a treasure trove of creativity at your fingertips.

Materials List

RECYCLED MATERIALS
CD
Function keys (salvaged from a defunct keyboard)
Clockworks (salvaged from a promotional clock)

TOOLS & SUPPLIES
Washer
Beadfix glue (Beadalon)

Step 1 The function keys can easily be pried off the computer. They're held in place by small plastic routainers. Leverage a fingernail or nail file under an edge and gently lift up. Remove the clockworks from the existing face. (In my case, this required pulling off the top pin that held the clock hands in place. I was then able to slide off the hour, minute and second hands. With the help of a small wrench, I released the nut that clamped the clockworks to the face. The small battery-powered clockworks, along with the empty post, slid easily off the back of the old clock face.)

Step 2 Thread a CD onto the freed post. Thread a washer onto the post to hold the CD in place. Rethread the nut and tighten it. Slide the clock hands back onto the post, starting with the second hand followed by the minute hand and ending with the hour hand. Finally, replace the top pin.

Step 3 Manually swivel the hands around the clock to mark the position of twelve, three, six and nine o'clock. Carefully glue the appropriate function key to each of those points. Apply a very small amount of glue to the outside edge of each key. Use caution, as the glue is very liquid and drips easily. Fill in the one, two, four, five, seven, eight, ten and eleven keys. It's important not to disturb any of the keys while they're drying, as they will instantly move and spread glue onto your clock face. Once the glue has dried, the connection is very strong. Replace the battery and hang your finished clock on the wall.

Frames often are refinished with tile paint, beads or sequins, but have you ever thought of covering one with aluminum cans? They're extremely lightweight, easy to cut with scissors and come printed with beautiful colors and designs. The aluminum also wraps easily around the frame and folds to tuck under the edges. Small wire nails tack the aluminum in place, a simple task if you prepunch the holes.

Materials List

RECYCLED MATERIALS
Assorted aluminum cans

OTHER MATERIALS
Flat wooden mirror frame
String or picture hanger

TOOLS & SUPPLIES
Scissors
Nail punch
Hammer
No.18 ⅝" (16mm) wire nails
Wire cutters
Eye screws

Aluminum Mirror Frame

Step 1 Cut the tops and bottoms off of the cans. Unroll the aluminum and lay flat.

Step 2 Select a square of aluminum and place it over a corner of the frame. Fold the metal along the vertical and horizontal edge. Cut a notch out of the metal so that it wraps around the corner. Prepunch holes with the nail punch, then hammer two nails to the outside edge on either side of the corner to anchor the metal.

Step 3 Fold under ⅛" (3mm) along one edge of a metal section to wrap around the mirror opening.

Step 4 Hook the bent metal around the mirror opening and pull the length of the metal across the front of the frame, wrapping it around the outside edge. Nail the piece in place along the outside edge of the frame. Continue adding new aluminum pieces in this fashion until you've covered the front of the frame. Setting nails around the edge is trickier as the glass is inset into the frame. Use wire cutters to clip the ends off the nails to shorten them to ⅜" (9mm). Use the nail punch to prepunch a hole on the edge of the frame where you want to position the first nail. Place a trimmed nail into the hole, and hammer it in place. Use this method to hammer two to three nails into each metal section around the edge.

Step 5 Cover the back of the frame with your aluminum scraps. Use shortened nails and the prepunch method to tack the metal sections in place. Affix eye screws and string or a hanger to the back to hang.

The New Yorker was the inspiration for this unique trash basket. The sporadic colored cartoons pop out of the simple black-and-white, text-rich pages. Like the *Glossy Magazine Bowl* (see pages 72–74), printed paper strips are repeatedly folded to create a stronger building material. In this case, four paper strips are folded together to make each square. The squares are hot glued together to make the base and sides of the basket. Four single rolled pages form each corner of the basket. Strips are glued around the top edge to help strengthen the basket. If you don't want to commit to a whole bowl or basket, you can stop either project at coaster size.

Black & White Magazine Basket

♲ What a Green Idea!

Do your part to eliminate paper waste. Visit www.41pounds.org, a nonprofit organization that helps stop the flow of unwanted junk mail.
    Find more seasonal ideas in *Living the Green Life* on pages 102–103.

Materials List

RECYCLED MATERIALS
Black and white or text-heavy magazines

TOOLS & SUPPLIES
Glue gun and glue sticks
Mod Podge
Glue brush

RESOURCES
Finished size: 11" × 7½" (28cm × 19cm)

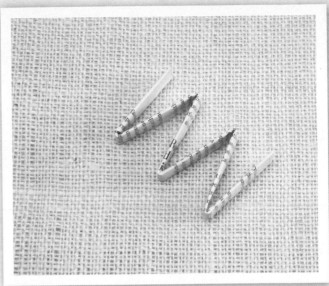

Step 1 Rip predominately black-and-white pages from the magazines. Save the covers for the corner supports. Fold each page into strips according to Steps 4–6 in the chip bag tote (see pages 52–55). This folding technique traps the edges inside the strip. Then fold the strip in half lengthwise twice. The first folds will help create a smoother wrong side edge.

Step 2 Accordion fold the strip every 1½" (4cm). You'll need four folded pieces for each square, nine squares for the base and twelve squares for each of the five rows up the basket, for a total of 276 pieces.

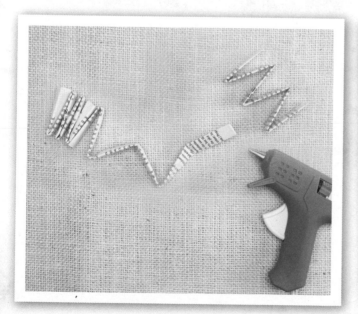

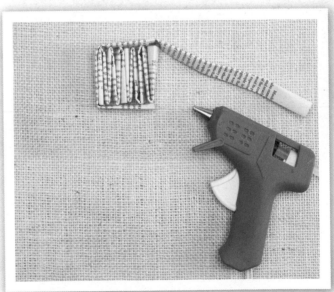

Step 3 Using a small amount of hot glue, loosely tack the inside folds of one strip together and then attach a second strip to the outside and glue its folds in place. This will create the inside of your first square.

Step 4 Hot glue a third strip around the outside edge of your two inside pieces. Use the fold lines to created the corners of the square.

MORE STEPS ➤

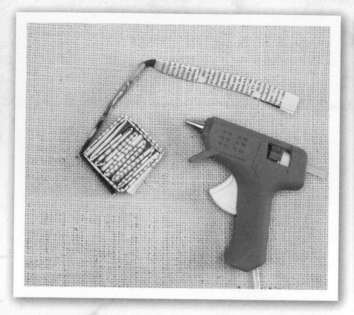

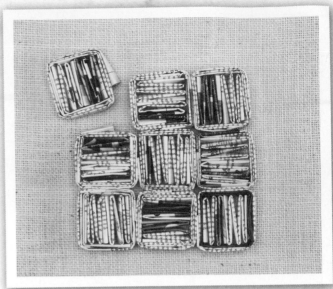

Step 5 Add a second wrapping strip around the outside of the square, continuing to match the fold lines to the corners. This will work until you reach the end of the strip where the extra bulk will force you to glue the end halfway down one side. Repeat the process to assemble your squares.

Be sure to work the right side up, facing the single fold side of the strips up when assembling the squares. The two-edge side will be the wrong side and will fall into the underside and inside of the basket.

Step 6 Arrange three rows of three squares to create the base. Rotate the squares to alternate the direction on the inside strips. For example, the first row would be horizontal, vertical, horizontal. The next row would be vertical, horizontal, vertical.

Tip
Try to place the sides with the partial outer strips (sides with a strip only halfway down the side) on the inside. This will ensure that the outside edges are uniformly smooth.

Step 7 To strengthen and enlarge the base, hot glue five rows of straight strips (strips that haven't been accordion folded) from Step 1 around the outside of the nine squares.

Step 8 To glue your first row in place, hot glue three squares to each side of the base, positioning them directly over the strips you just finished wrapping and gluing in place. Keep three things in mind while gluing: Make sure the single fold faces out, alternate the direction of the center folds (vertical/horizontal) and position the partial ends on the inside.

Step 9 The top, bottom and inside connections will all have direct strip-to-strip contact. The outside corners are different. Only the inside edges of the squares will touch. This connection isn't as secure but it leaves room to add rolled supports later (Step 10). Continue working your way up the basket until you've completed five rows.

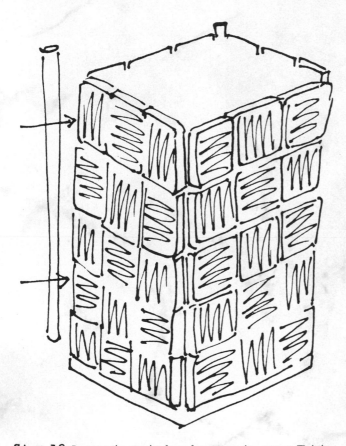

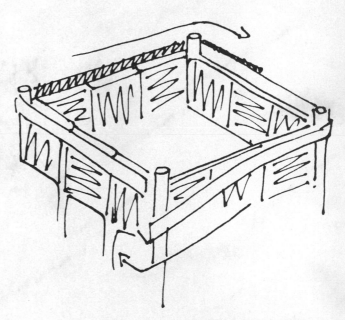

Step 10 Remove the staples from four magazine covers. Tightly roll each cover, starting at the back cover and ending at the outside edge of the front cover. Apply a line of hot glue under the edge to secure the roll. Hot glue each rolled cover to a corner of the basket.

Step 11 The rolled covers will extend slightly above the last row. Wrap and glue two rows of straight strips around the top of the basket. These strips will help strengthen the top of the basket. Apply a protective coat of Mod Podge to both the inside and outside of the finished basket.

If you're someone who holds on to pencil stubs and has children who collect new colored pencil sets each school year, here's a whole new way to utilize your extra supplies. The pencils are taped together and sawed to the same length with a single cut. Then they're drilled and strung together on heavyweight elastic cord. You can either recycle an old watch face or buy a new one at your local craft store. Wooden bead dangles match the colored pencils and dress up the finished piece.

Materials List

RECYCLED MATERIALS
Colored pencils

OTHER MATERIALS
Large crimp tubes
Square watch face (Beadalon)
Two 11" (28cm) sections of 1mm
    clear elastic jewelry cord
Silver bead caps (Blue Moon)
Wooden beads
Headpins

TOOLS & SUPPLIES
1"-wide (3cm) masking tape
Band saw
Drill
Crimping pliers
Round nose pliers
Wire cutters
Mod Podge Furniture Hard Coat
    (Plaid)

Colored Pencil Watch Strap

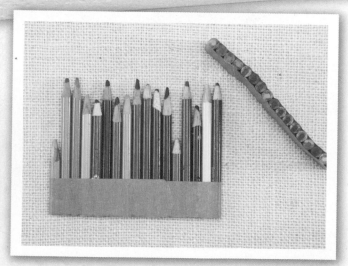

Step 1 Line the pencils side by side along a length of masking tape. Fold the tape over the last pencil and press it down across all the pencils. Wrap the end under the first pencil. Use the top and bottom edges of the tape as your guide to cut the pencils with a band saw.

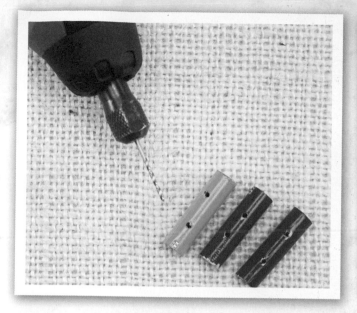

Step 2 Remove the tape and drill two holes in each pencil piece ¼" (6mm) from the top and bottom. (We did this while the pencils were still covered in tape and found that some of the outside color came off with the tape.)

Step 3 Use crimping pliers to crimp one end of each elastic strand to the outside holes on one side of the watch face. You may need to stretch the elastic inside the crimp tube to allow more room to thread the end back through before crimping it flat. Begin stringing the pencil pieces onto the elastic.

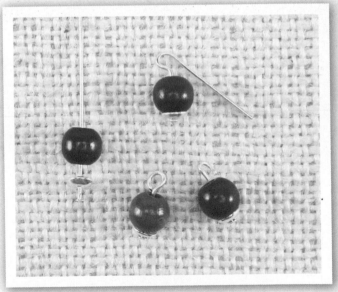

Step 4 Test fit the pencil watchband around your wrist to determine how many pencil pieces fit comfortably (our sample has twenty pencil pieces). Once you're pleased with the band, crimp the other end of the elastic strands to the other side of the watch.

Step 5 String a bead cap and a wooden bead onto a headpin. Use round nose pliers to shape the headpin and wire cutters to trim the end. Hook it onto the center hole on the side of the watch face. Wrap the wire end around the base of the loop and trim the end. Repeat the process three times to add a total of two beaded headpins to either side of the watch.

This **funky disco** ball repurposes a small stack of compact discs. Not your generic party light, there's a Nerf ball at the core. The ball's surface is covered with irregular shards of hand-cut compact discs. When I hung it to dry in the dining room, my efforts were rewarded. The sunlight streaming in the window sent hundreds of rainbow prisms all over the room. My daughter and I immediately started our celebratory craft dance.

CD Disco Ball

Project Note

I read somewhere that you can break apart a CD with a hammer, mosaic fashion. I found this to be an exercise in futility, as it shattered the mirrored surface without actually breaking the CD apart. I also discovered that some CDs are easier to cut than others, depending on how they are labeled.

Materials List

RECYCLED MATERIALS

Compact discs
Wooden handle from a damaged foam paint-brush, or a 5" (13cm) section of ½" (1cm) wood dowel
Nerf basketball

TOOLS & SUPPLIES

Drill
Eye screw
Craft glue
Fishing line
Paintbrush
Silver acrylic paint
Scissors
Aleene's 7800 All-Purpose Adhesive

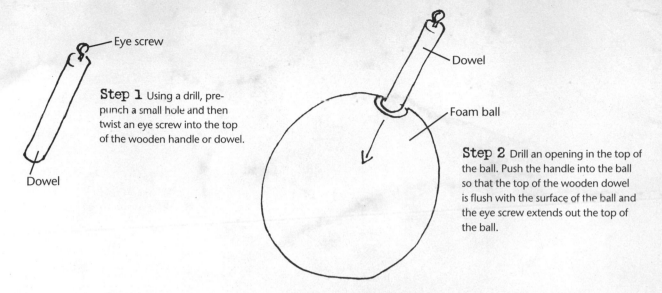

Eye screw

Step 1 Using a drill, pre-punch a small hole and then twist an eye screw into the top of the wooden handle or dowel.

Dowel

Dowel

Foam ball

Step 2 Drill an opening in the top of the ball. Push the handle into the ball so that the top of the wooden dowel is flush with the surface of the ball and the eye screw extends out the top of the ball.

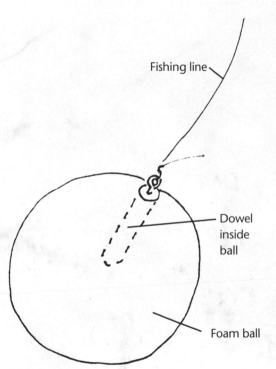

Fishing line

Dowel inside ball

Foam ball

Step 3 Pull out the dowel, apply craft glue and reinsert. Let it dry. After the glue has dried, thread a generous length of fishing line through the eye screw and suspend the ball over your workspace. Brush the ball with a layer of silver paint and let dry.

Step 4 With scissors, carefully cut into a CD. First cut out the center clear plastic section, then cut the remaining silver material into sections that are 1" (3cm) or smaller. You'll probably need pieces from five or six CDs to mirror your ball.

Step 5 Cover the surface of your prepainted ball with the CD shards. Apply Aleene's 7800 All-Purpose Adhesive to the back of each CD shard before you position it on the ball. Try to keep the surfaces clear of glue as it will mar the finished ball. It's a good idea to start in one section and build out, placing pieces as close together as possible. Keep the scissors on hand as you might need to trim some pieces to get a closer fit. Let the glue dry completely.

Step 6 Hang your finished disco ball where it will be illuminated from a direct light source.

Graphic design is everywhere, including our morning cereal boxes. Have you ever stopped to consider how beautiful all the printed colors are? Instead of tossing them into your recycling bin, you can preserve the colors and make a new container. A paper trimmer cuts the boxes down into uniform strips. Hot glue joins the strips end to end to increase their length. Rows of prepared strips are lined up and woven together to make a beautiful catch-all for your counter or desktop.

Cereal Box Basket

What a Green Idea!

Help reduce the harvesting of timber for disposable paper goods by switching to cloth napkins and towels in the kitchen, and buying toilet paper made with recycled fabrics. When you shop for back-to-school supplies, buy recycled paper products.

Find more seasonal ideas in *Living the Green Life* on pages 102–103.

Materials List

RECYCLED MATERIALS
Assortment of different colored cereal, popsicle and cracker boxes

TOOLS & SUPPLIES
Scissors
Paper cutter
Glue gun and glue sticks
Mod Podge (Plaid)
Glue brush

RESOURCES
Finished size: 5½" × 5½" × 5¾"
    (14cm × 14cm × 15cm)

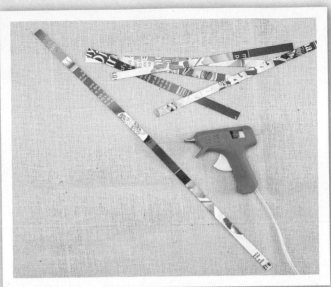

Step 1 Use scissors to cut open the boxes. Cut off the sides and the top and bottom flaps, leaving the front and back of each box intact. Place a flat cardboard piece in the paper cutter and cut the box into ¼" wide (6mm) pieces.

Step 2 Use a small dot of hot glue to connect ⅛" (3mm) of one strip end over another strip end. You'll need eighteen of these double-length strips to assemble the base (see Step 3) and another eight of them to weave up the sides (see Step 5).

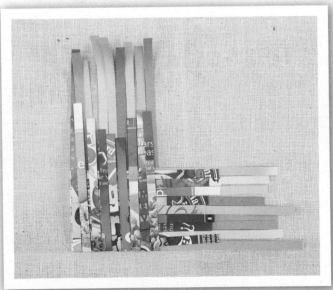

Step 3 Line up nine strips (right side up) vertically, deliberately distributing box varieties and colors. Weave another nine strips horizontally over and under the center of the vertical strips. Shift the overlapped connections so they're directly over or under another piece. If they're in between, the added bulk will prevent a tight weave.

Step 4 Turn the piece over (wrong side up). Working on one side at a time, fold the strips up over the woven section. Make sure the folds line up to make a straight edge to the base. Then crease the folds with your fingertip. Repeat with the remaining three sides.

MORE STEPS ➤

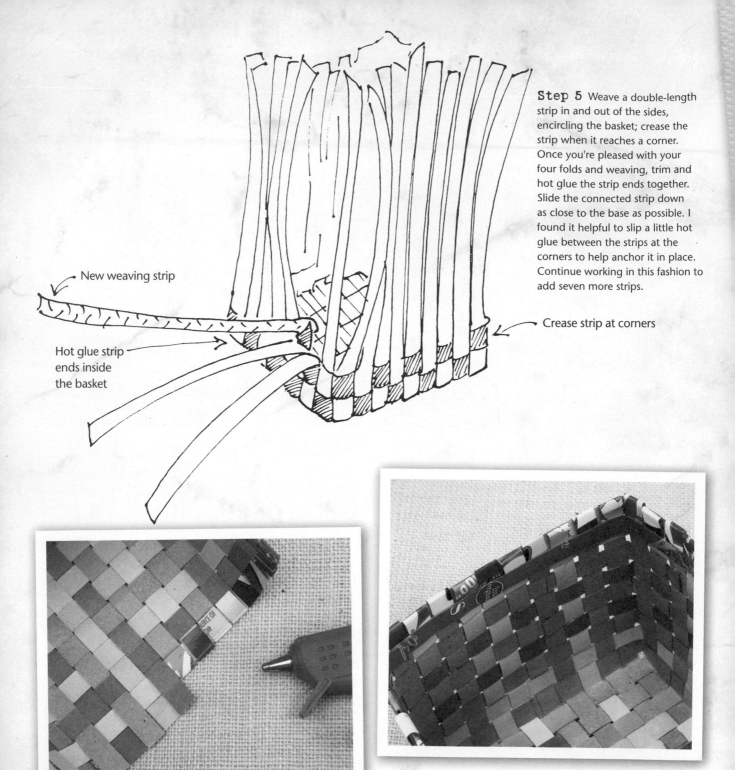

Step 5 Weave a double-length strip in and out of the sides, encircling the basket; crease the strip when it reaches a corner. Once you're pleased with your four folds and weaving, trim and hot glue the strip ends together. Slide the connected strip down as close to the base as possible. I found it helpful to slip a little hot glue between the strips at the corners to help anchor it in place. Continue working in this fashion to add seven more strips.

New weaving strip

Hot glue strip ends inside the basket

Crease strip at corners

Step 6 Trim each vertical strip ¾" (19mm) from the top of the last woven horizontal strip. Fold each end down into the basket and hot glue it in place.

Step 7 Hot glue a strip over the base of the glued strip ends to conceal the connections. Continue working your way around the basket adding a second strip and trimming the end when you've finished. Finally, coat both the inside and outside of the box with a protective coat of découpage medium.

Step 2 Use scissors to cut the vinyl covering off the binder. You'll need the salvaged cardboard spine, front cover and back cover to make your new binder. Next, cut open the vinyl album cover so that you have a single thickness of cardstock for the front cover and back cover. Repeat the process with the record sleeve so that you have two separate pieces of lightweight paper. Use the salvaged binder covers as pattern pieces by laying them over the separated album covers and tracing around the edges. Then repeat the process to trace them onto the record sleeve paper. Carefully cut along the lines. This will give you two outside covers made from cardstock and two inside covers made from the record sleeves.

Step 3 Brush acrylic paint to the outside edges of the salvaged binder covers and let dry. Use craft glue to adhere the album covers to the outside of the binder covers. Use a thin layer of glue to attach the record sleeve papers to the inside of the covers. Smooth any wrinkles and, if necessary, apply additional glue to the edges to reinforce the connection.

Step 4 Brush a protective coat of Paper Mod Podge over the front and back covers. After the clear coat dries, you can apply a coat to the inside covers. I found that the wax content in the record sleeve paper caused the paper to ripple. I removed the ripples with a heat gun, but you may want to spare yourself the frustration and leave the inside papers untreated.

Step 5 Iron interfacing to the back side of your fabric. Remove the paper backing after the fabric has cooled. Use a rotary cutter, mat and ruler to trim the fabric so that it's 4½" (11cm) wide. You'll need to increase that measurement for binders larger than 1" (3cm). Cut the fabric so that it's long enough to completely wrap the front and back of the salvaged binder spine; in my case, that was 24" (61cm).

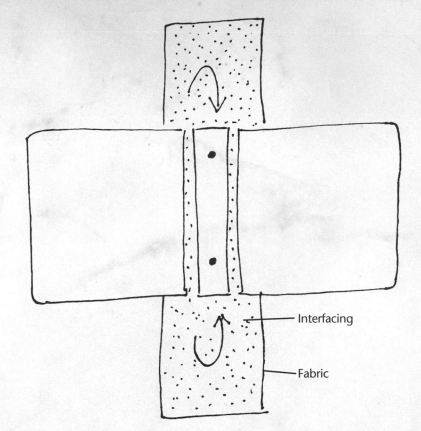

Interfacing

Fabric

Step 6 Lay the fabric right side down onto your work surface. Center the salvage spine in the middle of the fabric. Position the outside covers ¼" (6mm) out from either side of the spine. Temporarily remove the pieces and apply a generous amount of craft glue to the entire center of the fabric, then replace the spine and covers. Apply more glue to the fabric that extends above and below the spine and covers. Fold the fabric up and over the spine so that it completely envelops the spine and inside edges of the cover. Run you finger down either side of the spine to adhere the two layers together. Allow the glue to dry completely.

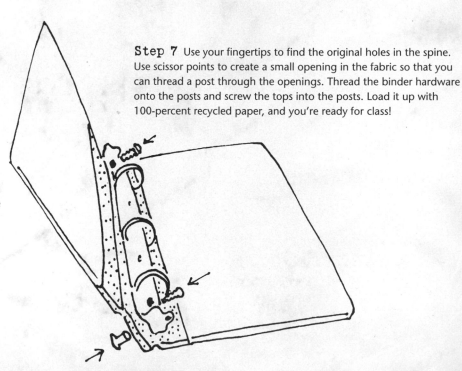

Step 7 Use your fingertips to find the original holes in the spine. Use scissor points to create a small opening in the fabric so that you can thread a post through the openings. Thread the binder hardware onto the posts and screw the tops into the posts. Load it up with 100-percent recycled paper, and you're ready for class!

I've always admired my friend Hannah's garlic dryer. It hangs from her windowsill away from moisture. She purchased it several years ago at a craft fair. After close inspection, I realized it's crocheted out of raffia, the fronds of the palm tree. I like the idea of experimenting with a natural, renewable material, especially when the end result makes a breathable container to store the garlic harvest. Raffia isn't as easy to crochet with as conventional yarn is, but it is flexible and forgiving, and the constant addition of new strands creates an interesting texture.

Raffia Garlic Dryer

 ## What a Green Idea!

Institute a Sunday bake day, cooking a large piece of meat that you can transform into other meals during the week. Bake muffins and cookies at the same time, making total use of the energy spent on heating the oven.

Find more seasonal ideas in *Living the Green Life* on pages 102–103.

Materials List

OTHER MATERIALS
Raffia (a third of a bag or less makes one garlic dryer)

TOOLS & SUPPLIES
Crochet hook K 10.5

RESOURCES
Crochet Techniques: pages 134–135

Step 1 Hold two pieces of raffia together and crochet them as a single strand. Before you reach the last 4" (10cm) of your strands, grab two more pieces and crochet all four strands together. Once you've made a stitch or two, let the two ends stick out and continue crocheting with the new strands. Repeat the process each time you come near the end of your strands. Don't worry if the ends look uneven; you can give your bag a haircut after you're finished.

Step 2 Make a slipknot and then hook 4 stitches on a chain. Connect the last chain stitch to the first knot to make a loop.

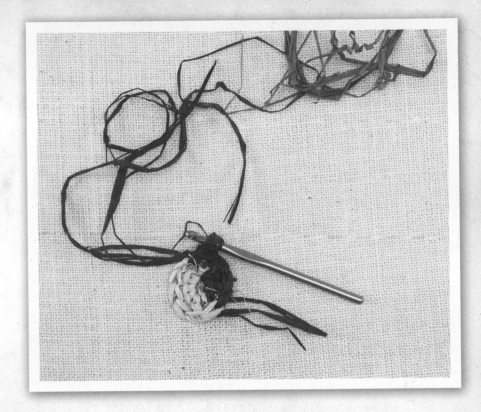

Project Note

Raffia is harvested from palm trees. It's a natural fiber that ages well and attractively stores garlic while allowing it to breathe. Raffia is also used to make garlic braids.

Step 3 Use the following pattern to crochet the dryer (see *Crochet Techniques*, pages 134-135):

a.) Row 1: Chain 2 and then make 8 double crochets around the loop created in Step 2. Connect to the second chain.

b.) Row 2: Chain 2 and then *double crochet in the first stitch and then make 2 double crochet in the second stitch*. Repeat the stitches listed between the asterisks all the way around the row to connect to the second chain (total of 14 stitches).

c.) Row 3: Repeat Row 2 (total of 21 stitches).

d.) Rows 4 and 5: Double crochet in each stitch for 21 stitches.

e.) Row 6: Make 2 double crochet in the first stitch and make 1 double crochet in the remaining 19 stitches for 23 stitches.

f.) Row 7: Repeat Row 6 for 25 stitches.

g.) Row 8: Double crochet in the next 6 stitches, then turn work. This will raise up the center back of the pouch.

h.) Row 9: Chain 1 and then make a single double crochet in stitches 3, 4 and 5 of Row 8. This will finish raising the center back of the pouch.

i.) Row 10: Make a single crochet around the entire top of the pouch, ending at the top of the raised portion. Chain stitches to the desired hanger length and then connect the chain alongside the last single crochet. Pull the ends through the loop and pull tight.

Ruler Chalkboard

This chalkboard rules! No more searching for paper and tape with this beautiful message board hung in the center of your home. All you need is a smooth scrap of wood and some chalkboard paint. (You can add a layer of magnetic paint, if you'd like to hang magnets from your board, too.) For our board, we had a sheet of masonite on hand. After the paint dried, Jon created a framework of salvaged yardsticks and glued them around the chalkboard.

Tip

Flea markets and hardware stores are great places to find wooden yardsticks.

Materials List

RECYCLED MATERIALS
Masonite board or smooth board plywood
Approximately 9 salvaged yardsticks

TOOLS & SUPPLIES
Chalkboard paint
Foam paint roller
Saw
Wood glue
Clamps or bricks for weights
Picture hangers

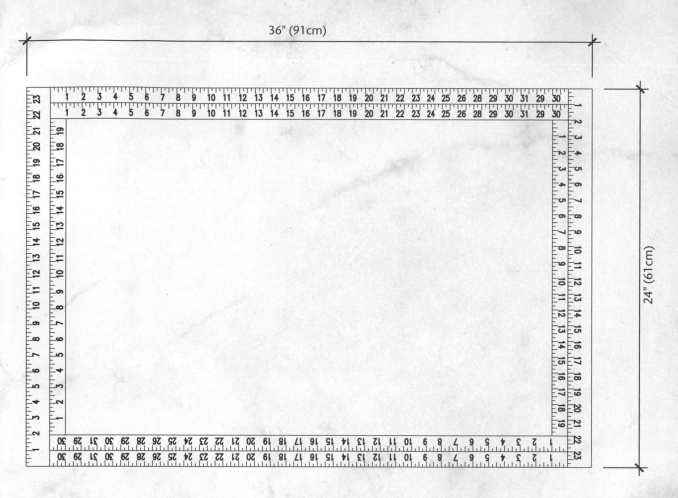

36" (91cm)

24" (61cm)

Diagram 1: Plan Detail

Step 1 Cut your masonite or board to the desired size. Take a moment to plan where you want to hang your board, and size it accordingly. Our board is 24" × 36" (61cm × 91cm). Also keep in mind that the bigger your board is, the more yardsticks you will need to frame it.

Step 2 Smooth several coats of chalkboard paint onto the board, letting each coat dry completely before applying the next.

Step 3 Lay the yardsticks around the perimeter of your board, planning which ones will need to be cut and where. We avoided cutting the yardsticks at an angle by butting the straight cut edges against each other. Once you've cut the yardsticks, apply a generous amount of glue to the underside and clamp or weight them in place while the glue dries.

Step 4 Attach picture hangers to the back side of the finished board.

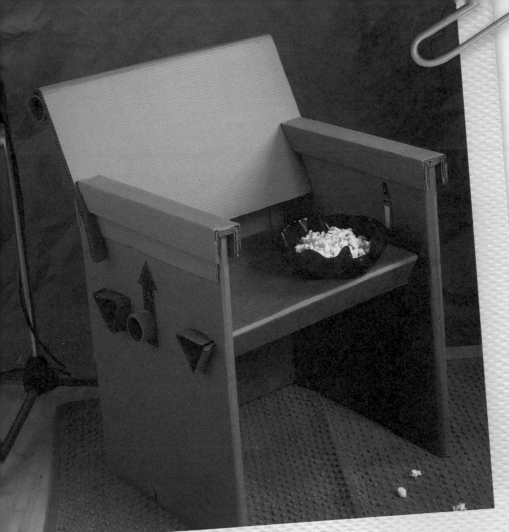

I love the idea of making something functional out of discarded packaging. Jon and I worked hard on this design to ensure that it could really support weight and be used as a chair. The cardboard has been folded and layered for extra strength. There are minimal cuts and connections that could add to wear and breakage. We found that heavy-duty cardboard tubes were the perfect seat supports. If you don't have any tubes, you can fold and glue additional triangle cardboard supports.

Corrugated Cardboard Chair

Materials List

RECYCLED MATERIALS
Three chair-sized corrugated cardboard boxes (check with your local furniture store)
Two heavy-duty cardboard tubes (check with companies who print on large rolls of paper)
Two U-shaped corrugated cardboard sleeves

TOOLS & SUPPLIES
Utility knife
Wood glue
Clamps and bricks for weights
Drill with hole saw attachment

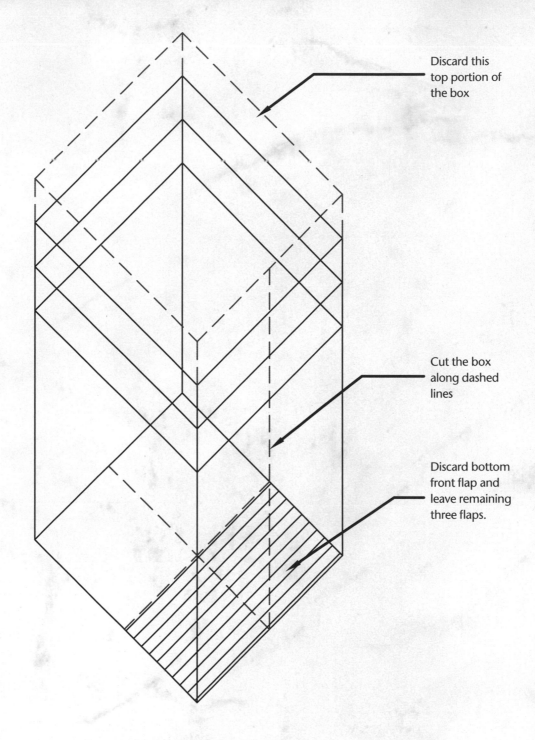

Discard this top portion of the box

Cut the box along dashed lines

Discard bottom front flap and leave remaining three flaps.

Diagram 1: Isometric View

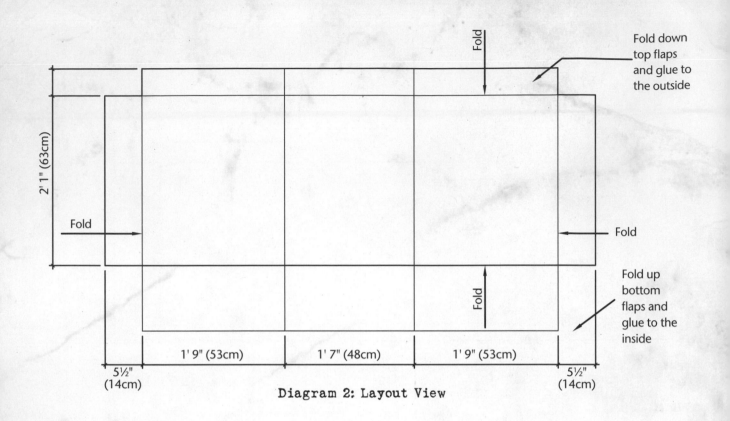

Fold

Fold down top flaps and glue to the outside

2' 1" (63cm)

Fold

Fold

Fold

Fold up bottom flaps and glue to the inside

1' 9" (53cm)   1' 7" (48cm)   1' 9" (53cm)

5½" (14cm)

5½" (14cm)

Diagram 2: Layout View

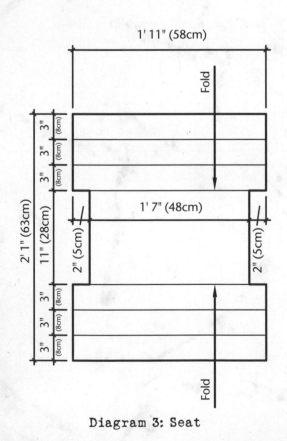

1' 11" (58cm)

Fold

3" (8cm)
3" (8cm)
3" (8cm)

1' 7" (48cm)

2' 1" (63cm)

11" (28cm)

2" (5cm)

2" (5cm)

3" (8cm)
3" (8cm)
3" (8cm)

Fold

Diagram 3: Seat

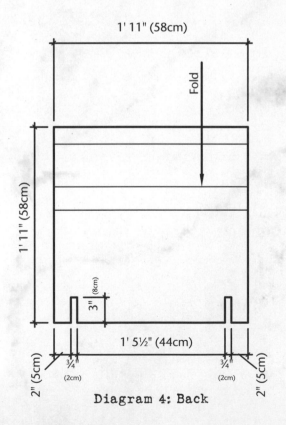

1' 11" (58cm)

Fold

1' 11" (58cm)

3" (8cm)

1' 5½" (44cm)

2" (5cm)

¾" (2cm)

¾" (2cm)

2" (5cm)

Diagram 4: Back

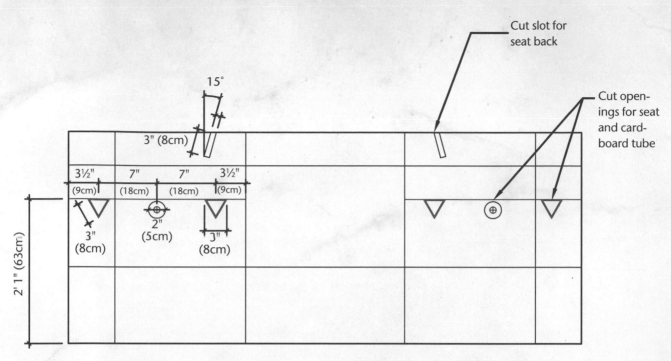

Diagram 5: Layout View

Step 1 Refer to Diagram 1 (page 99) to create the U-shaped chair base. Cut two boxes open down the middle on the front side. As shown in Diagram 2 (page 99), place one flattened box over the other. Remove the flaps from the top box. Fold the side flaps from the bottom box up and over the top box, then glue and weight them in place. Fold the top and bottom flaps up and over and glue them in place. Place weights over the glued sections while they dry. This will create a sturdy base for your chair.

Step 2 Cut two pieces for both the seat and the back, as shown in Diagrams 3 and 4 (page 100). Glue the layers together and place weights on them while they dry. Fold the flaps at the front and back of the seat into triangular prism shapes and glue. Use clamps to hold them in position while they dry. Roll the flap at the top of the chair back around a cardboard tube, and glue and clamp it in place while the glue dries.

Step 3 Refer to Diagram 5 (page 101) to cut triangular slots in the U-shaped chair base with a utility knife and make the round openings with a hold saw. Slot the triangle seat ends into the chair base, and then slide the tub seat support through the holes. Cut a diagonal slit and slide the chair back into the slots. Push the U-shaped armrests over the sides of the base.

Project Note

To build the same size chair as ours, refer to the diagrams for exact measurements. Feel free to modify the dimensions to work with the boxes you have. Avoid placing the folded box seams where they take direct pressure, especially in the seat area. The strength of the original box will determine the sturdiness of your finished chair.

Living the Green Life:
Ideas, Activities & Recipes

Eco Ideas

Autumn is the back-to-school season, so put on your thinking caps and consider ways to green your routine. Here are some ideas to get you started:

○ Organize a carpooling network with neighbors to help conserve fuel. This is the time of year that after-school activities swing into gear.

○ Instead of turning up the heat, wear an extra layer of clothing, warm socks and slippers. Keep a warm afghan on the couch to snuggle up with in the evenings.

○ Perform an energy audit. Contact your local energy provider. Most will perform an audit of your home for little or no cost, and it's money and time well spent. The resulting cost-benefit analysis will help you prioritize which projects you choose to do and give you an idea of payback. For instance, caulking and replacing leaky windows may cost twice as much as adding insulation to your walls, but it may pay for itself in energy savings in half the time.

○ Weatherproof in autumn. It helps save energy during the heating season. Install storm windows, seal gaps around windows and doors with caulking, and make sure you have enough insulation where it counts.

○ Prepare to defend against old man winter by making or installing thermal shades. They create a great thermal barrier to prevent cold drafts and stop the loss of radiant heat through windows, especially at night.

○ Tune up your car, and have your chimney and heating system checked so they all run efficiently and safely through the winter months.

Relax, Unwind & Unplug

Fall back into fall, and enjoy the good weather days, and even the colder ones, with these fun activities:

○ Plant in Autumn. It's a great time to enhance your landscaping with new trees and shrubs.

○ Enjoy the last few farmers markets and stock up on honey, maple syrup, pickles and jams to see you through the winter.

○ Break out the cards, dominos and board games in the evenings.

○ Host a pumpkin-carving party. You can roast the seeds and compost the guts.

Foods for the Season

Harvest time marks the end of the growing season. Black bean soup is the perfect catch-all for the last tomatoes, corn, peppers and squash to come out of the garden. Nothing takes the chill out of the air and warms your home like the sweet, spicy aroma of pumpkin bread and apple crisp baking in the oven. Cut and freeze any extra apples from an orchard trip, so you can make apple crisp all winter long.

BLACK BEAN SOUP

Some dishes conjure good memories. This one will always remind me of a delicious lunch with my crafty girlfriends. Catherine Matthews Scanlon is an excellent vegetarian cook and served this soup one September afternoon. Between bites, we grilled her for the details of the recipe. It was so good that I made it for my family the next week. You'll appreciate this great way to use the abundant supply of zucchini, summer squash and corn.

2 tablespoons olive oil
1 onion, diced
2 cloves of garlic, minced
7 mushrooms, quartered
4 green onions, sliced
1 red pepper, finely chopped
1 tomato, seeded and cubed
1 small summer squash, quartered and sliced
1 small zucchini, quartered and slice
2 cans black beans, rinsed and drained
2 quarts tomato juice
2 cups chicken broth
1 teaspoon cumin
Salt and pepper
2 ears fresh corn, kernels cut off the cob
¼ cup chopped cilantro

1. Heat the olive oil in a Dutch oven. Sauté onion and garlic. Add the mushrooms and cook for several minutes.
2. Add the rest of the vegetables (except for the corn) and sauté them until tender, approximately 5 minutes. Add the beans, juice, broth, cumin, salt and pepper.

3. Bring to a boil and partially cover. Simmer for 20 minutes.

4. Add the corn 10 minutes before serving, and toss in the cilantro just before dishing it into bowls.

o o o o o o o o o o o o o o o o o o

LEMON GARLIC BAKED FISH

It took me a long time to get comfortable cooking fish. Living in Iowa for the first decade of our marriage limited our accessibility to fresh fish. In Maine, fish is always in season and affordably priced. This surefire recipe will work on all kinds of white fish. Haddock and cod would be my top picks on the East Coast. It would work well with my in-laws' fresh Minnesota lake catch of walleye pike and northern. The recipe gives the fish a flavorful crunchy topping while keeping the flesh moist.

1 to 1½ pounds of white fish
¼ cup butter
1 cup breadcrumbs
2 tablespoons parsley
2 teaspoons lemon zest
½ teaspoon garlic powder

1. Preheat the oven to 350°F. Butter a glass baking dish.
2. Lay the fish in the baking dish.
3. Melt the butter and add the breadcrumbs, parsley, lemon peel and garlic powder, mixing well.
4. Spread the mixture over the fish.
5. Bake for 25 minutes or until the center of the fish is opaque and flakes apart.

o o o o o o o o o o o o o o o o o o

APPLE CRISP

My neighbor Claudia Brzoza turned up this recipe for the perfect crisp. I love its simplicity. There's no crust to mess with, just throw the fruit in the baking dish and spread the buttery crunchy topping on top. It's my go-to dessert whenever I have fresh berries or apples on hand. Claudia has even made it with strawberries and rhubarb in the spring.

4–6 cups peeled and sliced tart apples, such as
   Cortland (If you're using fewer apples, add 2 cups
   of mixed berries such as raspberries and blueberries)
¼ cup flour
¼ cup sugar
¼ teaspoon cinnamon

Topping
1 cup oats
½ cup butter
½ cup flour
½ cup brown sugar
½ cup sugar
Salt

1. Preheat the oven to 350°F. Butter a 9" × 9" square dish.
2. Combine the apples, flour, sugar and cinnamon in a mixing bowl. Toss so that the apples are covered. Place in prepared dish.
3. Place the topping ingredients in a food processor. Pulse until the butter is broken into small pieces and well incorporated. Pour and press the mixture onto the apples.
4. Bake 1 hour until the apples are bubbling and the crust is golden. Serve warm over ice cream.

o o o o o o o o o o o o o o o o o o

PUMPKIN BREAD

There's nothing like the smell of pumpkin bread cooking in the oven to make it feel like fall. This recipe makes three moist, delicious loaves so you can have one right away, another to keep in the fridge for breakfast and another to give to a friend. If you don't have enough loaf pans, make a dozen muffins and a single loaf.

1 15oz can pumpkin
4 eggs
½ cup vegetable oil
½ cup sweetened applesauce
⅔ cup water
2 cups white sugar
1 cup brown sugar
3½ cups all-purpose flour
2 teaspoons baking soda
1½ teaspoons salt
1 teaspoon ground cinnamon
1 teaspoon ground nutmeg
½ teaspoon ground cloves
½ teaspoon ground ginger

1. Preheat the oven to 350°F.
2. Grease and flour three 7" × 3" loaf pans.
3. In a large bowl, whisk together the pumpkin puree, eggs, oil, applesauce, water and sugars until well blended. In a separate bowl, combine the flour, baking soda, salt, cinnamon, nutmeg, cloves and ginger. Stir the dry ingredients into the pumpkin mixture until just blended. Pour into the prepared pans.
4. Bake for about 50 minutes. Loaves are done when a toothpick inserted in the center comes out clean.

Chapter 4
winter

Don't let the chilly air cool your spirits! This chapter features ways to keep you warm and spread holiday cheer. Enjoy quiet evenings at home, relaxing by the glow of your own hand-poured candle mugs. Wrap up in a cozy afghan to keep warm when you dial down your thermostat. Save more energy by using our handy space-saving indoor drying rack in your laundry room.

I'm often amazed how much waste is generated in holiday decorating. If you have the time, consider creating reusable decorations from used materials.

Cut worn dress shirts into triangles, iron the layers together and string them into a festive banner. Cover emptied matchboxes with paper and ribbon scraps to make precious shadowbox ornaments.

Take advantage of more unconventional recycling materials to make your holiday gifts. Felt old wool sweaters in your washing machine, then cut them apart and stitch the pieces together to make unique mittens, bags and decorative birds. Barbie shoes, old campaign pins and bottle caps are all ideal base materials for making unique jewelry gifts. Even old license plates can make great crafting material. One of my favorite projects is the license plate-covered mailbox. It gives new life to a rusted mailbox and reflects headlights to prevent snowplow collisions.

 What a Green Idea!

'Tis the season to be craftcycling! Making recycled gifts is a festive, fun indoor activity, and these gifts are perfect for a holiday gift exchange with family, friends or co-workers.

Find more wintertime activities in *Living the Green Life* on pages 128–129.

If you've ever hesitated before tossing a candle stub or crayon into the trash, this project will give you a reason to actively collect your wax remnants. You'll also need to salvage a tin can and a mug or teacup. The wax is melted in the can, tinted with a crayon and poured directly into the mug. This quick and easy project doesn't require molds or make a mess. It does yield a beautiful candle that won't drip wax when it burns. The mug can be reused and enjoyed when the candle is finished.

Candle Mugs

 What a Green Idea!

Use a holiday mug as the candleholder for an unplugged decoration. For holiday decorations requiring electricity, switch to LED lights. They use up to 90 percent less energy than conventional Christmas lights and they last longer.

Find more seasonal ideas in *Living the Green Life* on pages 128–129.

Materials List

RECYCLED MATERIALS
Mug
Tin can
Candle stubs or warped candlesticks
Crayon stubs (to add color)

OTHER MATERIALS
Wick
Essential oils

TOOLS & SUPPLIES
Two bamboo skewers
Two clothespins
Saucepan

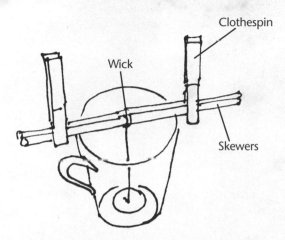

Clothespin

Wick

Skewers

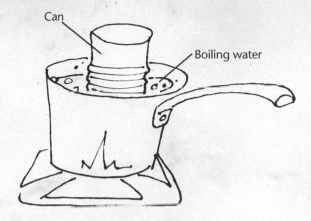

Can

Boiling water

Step 1 Lay one end of a candlewick in the base of a mug. Sandwich the top of the wick between two bamboo skewers to hold it up straight. Hold the skewers together with clothespins. Now your mug is ready for the wax.

Step 2 Fill a third of the pan with water and bring it to a boil on your stove top. Fill the tin can with wax. Don't worry about any imbedded wicks in the recycled candles. Stand the tin can in the boiling water. You may need to steady it with a wooden spoon or your hand, protected with an oven mitt. Once the wax has melted, remove any old candlewicks with a fork. Lay the salvaged wicks straight on wax paper. You should be able to reuse them after they've cooled and hardened. Add ¼" (6mm) or ½" (13mm) crayon into the wax to color it. If you're using a very opaque crayon, use less because the color is intensely saturated. Stir the mixture to integrate the color. If you're adding essential oils for scent, do it just after you take the wax off the heat.

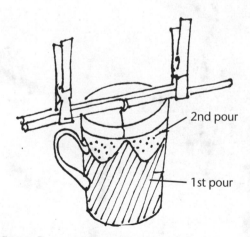

2nd pour

1st pour

Step 3 Carefully pour the wax into the pre-pared mug. Fill it all the way to the top. As the wax cools, it will sink. Save the remaining wax in the tin can so it will be ready to heat for a second pouring. Allow the wax-filled mug to cool completely.

Step 4 Reheat the water, replace the tin can and melt the remaining wax. Pour the melted wax over the first pouring to bring the candle level back to the top of the mug. Let the candle set overnight. Remove the clothes-pins and skewers and trim the wick.

It's no wonder Barbie's always losing shoes; it's hard to keep them on her tiny pointed feet. But her loss is our gain. Miniature doll shoes are playful inspiration for jewelry. Simply drill a hole through them, and they can be threaded with beaded eye pins or jump rings. I paired the shoe colors with a variety of shaped plastic beads from an assorted pack. A small length of rubber tubing gives the finished bracelet a simple, clean look. You could easily hang the shoes from a link bracelet or a beaded strand.

Miniature Doll Shoe Bracelet

Project Note

These miniature doll shoes make great earrings, too! Simply hook a drilled shoe onto a jump ring (see page 109, Steps 1 and 2). Next, hook an eye pin onto the ring. String a seed bead and a plastic flowered bead onto the eye pin. Trim and shape the end into a loop, and hook it onto the earring finding. Repeat for the second earring.

Materials List

RECYCLED MATERIALS
Miniature doll shoes

OTHER MATERIALS
19 strand .018" (0.5mm silver stringing wire (Beadalon)
10mm jump rings
Silver bumpers (Beadalon)
Plastic beads
6¼" (16cm) rubber tubing (Beadalon)
Lobster clasp
Crimp beads

TOOLS & SUPPLIES
Drill with ⅛" (3mm) bit
Beadfix glue (Beadalon)
Crimping pliers
Wire cutters

RESOURCES
Finished length: 8" (20cm)

Step 1 Drill a vertical hole through the back of the shoes.

Step 2 Open a jump ring laterally, and thread it through the drilled hole. Apply glue to the jump ring connection, and swivel the ring so that the connection is trapped inside the shoe. Squeeze glue into the drilled hole in the shoe. Let dry.

Step 3 With a crimp bead, attach one side of a lobster clasp to one end of the stringing wire.

Step 4 Begin stringing in the following sequence: silver bumper bead, plastic bead, silver bumper bead, rubber tubing.

Step 5 String the shoe onto the rubber tubing.

Step 6 String the following sequence: silver bumper bead, plastic bead, silver bumper bead.

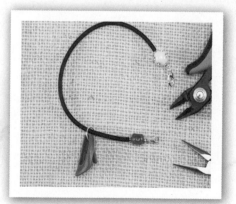

Step 7 With a crimp bead, attach the other end of the clasp to the end of the stringing wire.

Good old-fashioned cardboard matchboxes make an ideal frame for miniature odds and ends. The only restraint is finding something small enough to fit inside the removable inner tray. Doors and openings are cut out of the outer sleeve. Paper and ribbon scraps quickly conceal the box and instantly transform it into a piece of art. This project is perfect for a holiday art night with friends or a family crafting session. Each ornament takes on the character of the creator.

Matchbook Ornaments

Materials List

RECYCLED MATERIALS

Miniature toys or favors
Cardboard matchbook
Scraps of patterned paper
¼" wide (6mm) and ⅛" wide
    (3mm) ribbon scraps

TOOLS & SUPPLIES

Craft knife
Craft glue
Glue gun and glue sticks
26-gauge wire

Tip

Adapt this project to make tiny shrines showcasing treasures and collectibles year-round. Tiny keys and hearts for Valentine's Day, bunnies and eggs for Easter, even a spooky miniature haunted house for Halloween.

Step 1 Select the toy or favor you want to feature in your ornament and double-check that it will fit within the box. Slide the match tray out of the box. Select paper that complements the trinket. Trace around the outside of the tray, and cut out the rectangle. Glue it into the box. With a craft knife, cut a narrow paper strip and glue it around the inside and outside edge of the tray. Use a generous amount of craft glue to anchor heavier trinkets in the box; hot glue will work for lightweight, more porous objects.

Step 2 Let the finished tray dry while you work on the sleeve. Use a craft knife to cut a window in the front of the sleeve. Make a circle, rectangle or I-shaped cut that unfolds into two window shutters. Cover the remaining exposed matchbook with more paper or ribbon scraps.

Step 3 Slide the tray into the finished sleeve. Thread a hanging wire up through the center top of the tray or tray and sleeve (for horizontal shrines). Form the wire into a loop. Thread it back down and make a knot.

Blizzard Yarn Afghan

My friend Chesley had a wrap made out of cozy Blizzard yarn sitting on the couch in her store, The Knitting Experience Café. Day after day, she watched how her customers were lured to its warmth, weight and coziness. When I asked her to design a beginner's project for this book, she instantly knew what yarn to use. It's a heavy alpaca with just enough acrylic in it to make it washable. The entire afghan is knit in garter stitch, which means simple straight knitting with no purl stitches. To make the thick pink color squares, add a strand of pink to the brown, and then drop it to continue working in brown. As I write this on a cold winter night in Maine, I can't imagine anything more wonderful than wrapping up in this warm afghan and settling into a novel.

Step 1 Use the following pattern in Steps 1–8 to knit the afghan (see *Knitting Techniques*, pages 130-133): **a.)** Cast on 82 stitches using your main color. **b.)** Knit 20 rows.

Step 2: Begin color blocks. **a.)** Row 1: Knit 10 stitches, holding one strand of the contrast color along with the main color. Knit 14 stitches, drop the contrast color and knit 10 stitches in the main color. Join another ball of the contrast color, and holding the contrast color with the main color, knit 14 stitches, drop the contrast color and knit 10 stitches in the main color. Join another ball of the contrast color, and holding the contrast color with the main color, knit 14 stitches, drop the contrast color and knit 10 stitches in the main color. **b.)** Repeat Row 1 twenty-four times. Each time you come to a color

block, pick up the contrast color strand and hold it together with the main color. Drop the contrast color when you reach the end of each square and continue with the main color to the next block.

Step 3: Knit 20 rows in the main color.

Step 4: Repeat color blocks (Steps 2a and 2b).

Step 5: Knit 20 rows in the main color.

Step 6: Repeat color blocks (Steps 2a and 2b).

Step 7: Knit 20 rows in the main color.

Step 8: Bind off loosely and weave in the ends.

Materials List

MATERIALS
Reynold's Blizzard yarn (65% alpaca, 35% acrylic): nine skeins in main color (brown #118), two to three skeins in contrast color (pink #641)

TOOLS & SUPPLIES
40" (102cm) size US 15 circular needles

RESOURCES
Project Note: Gauge: 9 stitches × 13 rows = 4" (10cm) on US 15 needles in garter stitch.
Knitting Techniques: 130–133
Finished size: 39½" × 38" (100cm × 97cm)

Altered Pins

If **election or** advertising pins are cluttering up your dresser, here's a way to turn them into timeless art objects. Simply découpage a fabric scrap over the pin and embellish it with a cut paper shape and metal scrapbook charm. Spiraled wire and rhinestones add sheen and sparkle. Platinum bond glue ensures that all the elements are firmly attached so that your pin can be worn on coats and tote bags.

Materials List

RECYCLED MATERIALS
Fabric scraps
Pins
Pages from an old book
Scrapbook paper scraps

OTHER MATERIALS
Metal charms
Rhinestones
20-gauge wire

TOOLS & SUPPLIES
Wax paper
Mod Podge (Plaid)
Glue brush
Aleene's Platinum Bond Glass and
    Bead glue
Scissors
Flush cutters
Pliers

RESOURCES
Patterns: page 140

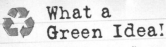

What a Green Idea!

When you personalize your pins with old photos, scraps of letters or notes, or other sentimental items, they become great gifts. Recycle comics, children's drawings and fabric into wrapping paper, and use it to wrap your pins.

Find more seasonal ideas in *Living the Green Life* on pages 128–129.

Step 1 Cut a piece of fabric that will cover a pin, and wrap it around the underside. Working over wax paper, brush Mod Podge over the top of the pin, smoothing the fabric over the glue.

Step 2 Flip the pin over and brush glue around the outer edge, avoiding the workings of the pin. Press the fabric edges down into the glue, and apply another coat of glue over the fabric to hold it in place. Brush two more coats of Mod Podge over the front and back of the pin.

Step 3 Using the patterns on page 140 as your guide, cut birds, butterflies or branches out of scrap paper.

Step 4 Use pliers to bend wire into the desired shape.

Step 5 Arrange cut paper, wire, rhinestones and charms over the pin. When you're pleased with the arrangement, use Mod Podge to glue onto the paper and platinum bond glue to attach the wire charms and rhinestones.

The simplicity of this purse's design is what initially captured my interest. The bag and handles are cut at the same time from a single sweater. Stitching up the base and folding the handles was a cinch. I embellished the front with colorful scraps cut into circles and squares. Decorative stitching holds the pieces in place while making this an accessory that doesn't go anywhere unnoticed. (For other felted wool projects, see *Sweet Sweater Birds*, page 118, and *Felted Sweater Mittens*, page 122.)

Felted Sweater Purse

Project Note

Felted sweaters are simply wool sweaters than have gone through the washing machine and dryer. The soap, water, heat and agitation pulls the individual wool fibers together so that the material shrinks. Felted wool is strong and thick, and doesn't fray at the edges when it's cut. I like to find sweaters at Salvation Army and Goodwill; the key is to look for those that are 100-percent wool. Some mohair work, just stay away from acrylic blends because they won't shrink.

Materials List

RECYCLED MATERIALS
Felted sweater (turquoise)
Scraps of felt to match the embroidery threads
(brown, mustard, red, green, turquoise, lavender, pink)

OTHER MATERIALS
Large button
Embroidery thread (white, brown, purple, pink, turquoise, ochre)

TOOLS & SUPPLIES
Scissors
Sewing machine
Sewing and darning needle

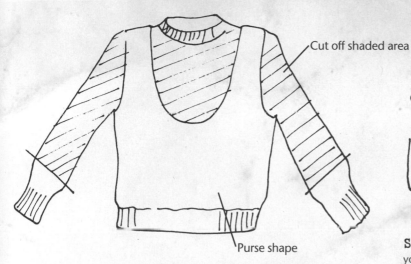

Cut off shaded area

Purse shape

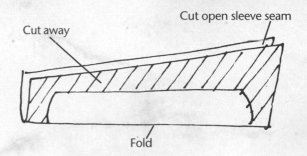

Cut away

Cut open sleeve seam

Fold

Step 1 Lay a felted sweater flat on your work surface. Following the diagram above, cut through both thicknesses to remove the sleeves and deepen the neck opening. Open the shoulder seams and remove excess fabric so the edges are a single thickness. Turn the sweater inside out. Cut the cuffs off the sleeves and save them to make *Felted Sweater Mittens* (page 122). Use one of the remaining sleeves to make the base of the purse (see Step 2) and save the other sleeve for mitten parts or birds (see page 118).

Step 2 Cut apart the length of the sleeve seam you're using for the purse base. Open it and trim away any excess fabric so you're left with a flat single thickness of felt. Fold it in half and trim the side edges so that the base is the same length as the sweater width. Trim the top and bottom edges so that they're straight. Trim away more fabric for a thinner base and less if you'd like a wider base.

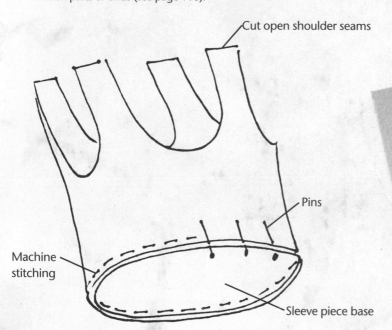

Cut open shoulder seams

Pins

Machine stitching

Sleeve piece base

Step 3 Unfold the trimmed base and position it in the bottom of the sweater, right side facing in. Pin it in place. Machine stitch around the base, removing pins as you work. Trim excess fabric off the corners, and turn the bag right side out.

Project Note

For felted fabric projects, outfit your sewing machine with a heavy-duty needle. Loosen the tension to accommodate the bulk of the fabrics. Run a double thickness test piece through the machine and make adjustments before sewing your bag.

MORE STEPS ▶

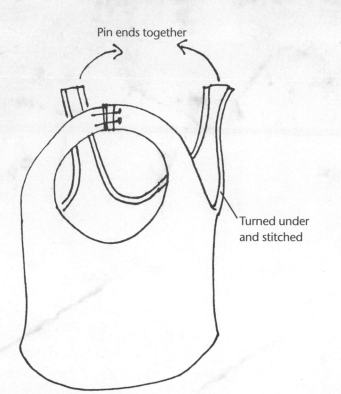

Pin ends together

Turned under
and stitched

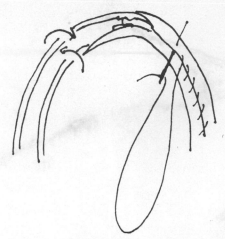

Step 5 To form the handles into a rolled shape, hand stitch them together, trapping all the machine seams inside the handle.

Step 4 To strengthen the edges of your purse, turn under ¼" (6mm) of fabric. Make a continuous seam, stopping only at the tops of the handles. To make a circular handle, connect the straps from the same side of the purse with a single seam.

Step 6 Cut twenty 2" × 2" (5cm × 5cm) squares and 1½" (4cm) circles out of your felt scraps. Stack the circles over the squares and arrange them into four rows of five pairs across the front of your bag. Distribute the colors among the rows and avoid pairing the same colors together. Leave the circle off the middle square of the top row, temporarily place a button in this spot and check your color distribution a final time. Use straight pins to anchor the circles and squares to the front of the bag.

Step 7 Thread a darning needle with a full strand of embroidery floss, and begin stitching up through the squares and sewing the circles in place. Alternate whip-stitching (see *Embroidery Techniques*, page 136) around the edges of some of the circles and spoking large stitches out from the center of others. Select floss colors that contrast with the color of the felt so that your stitchwork will be noticeable. Use smaller running stitches around the edges of the squares to anchor them in place.

Step 8 Stitch the button through the middle square (with no circle) and purse front several times to firmly anchor it in place. Cut 6½" × 1" (16cm × 3cm) strip of turquoise from your scraps. Hand stitch the edges together to give the strip a rolled appearance and added strength. Fold the strip in half to form a loop. Tuck the ends under and stitch them to the inside top of the purse back. Test fit the loop around the button before stitching it in place. You may need to trim ends to shorten the loop. I sewed partway down the center of the loop to narrow the hole for a tighter fit around the button.

Time to roll up your sleeves and make a no-sew banner that recycles worn shirts and celebrates the season. Each triangular pennant is cut from sleeves, giving you a double layer of fabric with a top fold. Iron-fusible interfacing between the layers holds them together, leaving the top fold open so that the letters can be strung together into a message. Additional fusible webbing irons letters to the base triangle.

Materials List

RECYCLED MATERIALS
Cotton shirts
Patterned fabric scraps

OTHER MATERIALS
Heat N' Bond interfacing
Stiff felt

TOOLS & SUPPLIES
Scissors
Fabric glue
Pinking sheers
Iron and ironing board

RESOURCES
Patterns: page 140–141

Holiday Sleeve Banner

Step 1 Cut the sleeve off a shirt, then cut the cuff off the sleeve. Cut a piece of Heat and Bond to fit inside the sleeve, narrowing it by 1" (3cm) so there's a ½" (13mm) gap between the Heat and Bond and the top and bottom folds in the sleeve. Position the Heat and Bond in the sleeve. Use the iron to bond the interfacing to the shirt. Reach in and remove the paper lining, and apply more heat to finish bonding the two layers of the sleeve together.

Step 2 Trace triangles (see pattern, page 140) onto the sleeve. Alternate positioning the flat edges against the top and bottom sleeve folds. Cut the pennants out

with pinking sheers.
Iron Heat and Bond to the back of your patterned fabric scraps. Trace the letter patterns (see page 141) onto the paper backing in reverse so they'll be correctly oriented when the right side of the fabric is showing.

Step 3 Cut the smaller triangles out of stiff felt or contrasting colored fabric. Peel the paper backing off the letters and position them on the smaller pennants. Iron them in place to activate the adhesive. Use fabric glue to attach the felt letter pennants to the sleeve pennants. Thread the assembled pennants (in order) onto a generous length of ribbon.

Tip
If you have large letter stamps, brush acrylic paint over the stamp and print a letter onto a plain piece of fabric. After the paint dries, use fusible webbing to iron the stamped letter onto your triangle piece. Make additional letters to change your message to fit any occasion. Both *love* and *peace* are quick and easy banner messages that work all year.

Birds of a sweater flock together. These charming little fellows make fabulous holiday gifts, but feel free to enjoy them all year long poised on a mantle or shelf. The body is made with three pieces of fabric that can be machine stitched or hand sewn. The black bead eyes are pulled into the head with a couple of stitches. Decorative embroidery floss stitches join the wings to either side. The wire legs are made with a single wire length that is poked across the bottom of the bird. Once you see how easy it is to make one, you might just decide to sew a whole flock.

Sweet Sweater Birds

Materials List

RECYCLED MATERIALS
Felted sweater scraps (For short tail: green, turquoise, burgundy. For long tail: tangerine, green, burgundy.)

OTHER MATERIALS
Black *E* beads
Stuffing (Nature-fil)
18-gauge wire
Embroidery floss (turquoise, pink, fuchsia)

TOOLS & SUPPLIES
Straight pins
Scissors
Sewing and darning needles
Thread (green, burgundy, black)
Flush cutters
Beadfix glue (Beadalon)
Glue gun and glue sticks
Sewing machine (optional)

RESOURCES
Project Note: page 114
Embroidery Techniques: pages 136–137
Patterns: pages 141

Step 1 Use the patterns (see page 141) as your guide to cut out two green sides and a turquoise stomach panel. Placing right sides together, pin the three pieces together. Position the one tip of the stomach panel at the neck and the other where the side tail points meet.

For the long-tail bird, the tail piece (see pattern, page 141) will extend beyond where the body pieces meet.

Leave an opening for stuffing

Step 2 Seam the stomach panel to each bird side. Stitch the two sides together starting at the neck, working over the top of the head and ending 1" (3cm) before the tail. Turn the bird right side out. Stuff the bird with fiberfill, pushing small amounts into the head and then filling the remainder of the body. Using matching green thread to hand stitch the tail opening closed.

Follow the same basic instructions for the long-tail bird, except place the extra tail piece in the opening before stitching it closed.

Step 3 Use the wing pattern (see page 141) to cut out two burgundy wings. Thread the darning needle with the full strand of embroidery thread and whipstitch (see *Embroidery Techniques*, page 136) the wings to the sides of the bird. Stitch an optional decorative swirl onto the center of each wing.

The long-tail bird doesn't have wings, so make decorative stitches on the sides.

Bend foot for stability

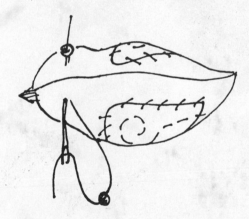

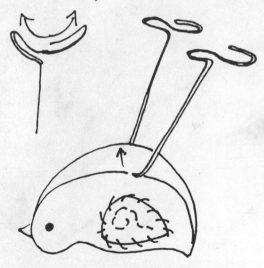

Step 4 Cut a small beak (see pattern, page 141) from the burgundy scraps and hot glue it into the seam that joins the front of the head together. Thread a sewing needle with black thread and stitch an *E* bead to either side of the head. Pass the needle back through the eyes several times to pull them into the head and hold them tightly in place.

Follow the same basic instructions for the long-tail bird.

Step 5 Working on the underside of the bird, poke wire end through the center panel and side seam. Push the wire across the inside of the belly, then poke it back out through opposite side of the panel. Pull 5½" (14cm) of wire out and fold both wires down where they emerge from the fabric. Shape each end into a 1" (3cm) N-shaped foot. Apply a spot of glue where the wire legs emerge from the bird's body.

For the long-tail bird, shorten the length of the legs before shaping the feet.

I love the look of cast resin bottle cap jewelry and even though I enjoy working with resin, sometimes I just want to craft something quick and easy without worrying about the fumes and mess. This kid-friendly project is the perfect solution. The message or image is cut from magazine pages (in this case *Rolling Stone*) glued inside the bottle cap and covered with a round bubble sticker. Liquid Beadz is smeared around the inside edge and voilà, instant jewelry!

Bottle Cap Necklaces

Materials List

RECYCLED MATERIALS
Metal bottle cap
Type and words cut
   from magazine
Ball chain necklace

OTHER MATERIALS
½"-¾" bubble stickers
Jump ring
Cardstock

TOOLS & SUPPLIES
Scrap of wood
Drill with 1/16" (1mm) bit
1" (3cm) circle punch (or trace a
   small lid and cut the circle by
   hand)
Aleene's Tacky glue
Pliers
Liquid Beadz (DecoArt)
Plastic knife or wooden craft stick

Step 1 Invert the caps onto a scrap piece of wood and drill a hole through the top of the metal. Position the hole between where the metal begins to curve and the rippled edge.

Step 2 Select words from magazines. Apply a very thin layer of glue to the back side of the page. Press the type over cardstock and let the glue dry. Carefully position the mounted words in the center of a punch and press out a circle.

Step 3 Use craft glue to mount the cut-out circle in the center of the inverted drilled bottle cap. Be sure to position it so that the hole remains unblocked. Firmly press a clear bubble sticker over the type.

Step 4 Carefully open a jump ring laterally with pliers and thread it through the hole. Close the ring so that the wire ends are flush.

Step 5 Use a plastic knife or wooden craft stick to smear Liquid Beadz around the edge of the bottle cap. Loop a ball chain necklace through the jump ring.

Felted Sweater Mittens

I love the idea of making a new wearable out of a worn garment, and these mittens do that with style. It takes four felted sweater pieces to make each mitten: a back, two inside pieces and a sleeve cuff. Mixing and matching the colors is half the fun. But what really makes this mitten design unique is the needle felted embellishment on the back. If you've never tried needle felting, you're in for a treat. Simply lay wool roving over the felted wool and use a barbed needle to poke it directly in place. With each prick, the tiny needle barbs blend the wool fibers together so they stick. You get instant results without threading a needle.

Materials List

RECYCLED MATERIALS
Felted sweater sleeves
Felted sweater cuffs

OTHER MATERIALS
Wool roving
Rigid insulation
Dark thread

TOOLS & SUPPLIES
Sewing machine
Felting needle (Clover)
Straight pins

RESOURCES
Project Note: page 114
Project Note: Wool roving is washed, carded and dyed wool that hasn't been spun. It is available at yarn and craft stores.
Patterns: page 142

 ## What a Green Idea!

Purchase seasonal sporting goods from a local ski and skate swap sale. If you don't have one in your area, see about organizing one and donating profits to environmental causes.

Find more seasonal ideas in *Living the Green Life* on pages 128–129.

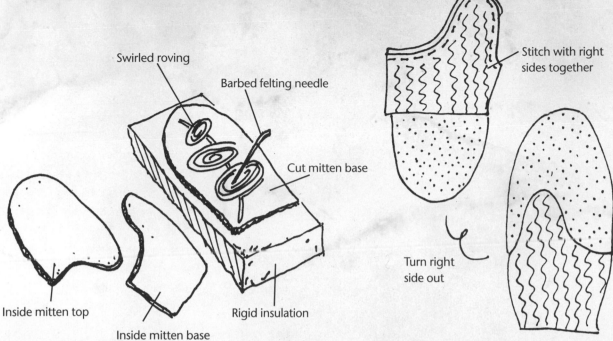

Swirled roving

Barbed felting needle

Cut mitten base

Inside mitten top

Inside mitten base

Rigid insulation

Step 1 Lay the mitten with its back right side up on your work surface. (I like to needle felt over rigid blue foam insulation scraps, but traditional dense foam will also cushion the back of your work, and protect both the needle tip and work surface.) Pull off a small strand of wool roving. Roll it into shape and position it over the mitten back. Work your needle up and down through the roving into the felt piece. The repetitive motion will compress the roving and integrate it into the felt. Repeat the process with the second mitten back.

Stitch with right sides together

Turn right side out

Step 2 Placing right sides together line the thumb of the inside mitten top (see pattern, page 142) with the thumb of the inside mitten base (see pattern, page 142). Stitch a single seam from one side of the mitten to the other to connect the two pieces of the thumb and the center of the mitten. Turn the thumb right side out.

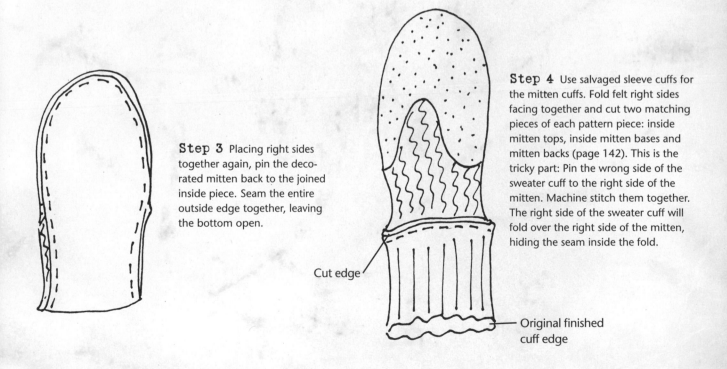

Step 3 Placing right sides together again, pin the decorated mitten back to the joined inside piece. Seam the entire outside edge together, leaving the bottom open.

Cut edge

Original finished cuff edge

Step 4 Use salvaged sleeve cuffs for the mitten cuffs. Fold felt right sides facing together and cut two matching pieces of each pattern piece: inside mitten tops, inside mitten bases and mitten backs (page 142). This is the tricky part: Pin the wrong side of the sweater cuff to the right side of the mitten. Machine stitch them together. The right side of the sweater cuff will fold over the right side of the mitten, hiding the seam inside the fold.

This easy-to-build space-saving drying rack hangs from the ceiling and can be raised and lowered as needed. My neighbor Claudia developed this rack to dry her handmade marbleized papers in her studio; we modified it for hanging clothing. You can either pin the clothes to the clothesline or hang them on a hanger and then loop the hanger onto the line. Hanging clothes up to dry not only saves energy, it also lengthens their lifespan and prevents excess shrinking. In a family of tall people, the latter benefit is my favorite.

Retractable Drying Rack

Project Note

No special stains or finishes are necessary for the wood in this project. We tinted the wood with diluted acrylic orange and purple paints.

Materials List

OTHER MATERIALS
Two 1" × 3" (3cm × 8cm) furring strips
Clothesline cord

TOOLS & SUPPLIES
Saw
Glue
Four eye screws
Drill with ¼" (6mm) bit
Orange and purple acrylic craft paint
Paintbrush
Waterproof sealer

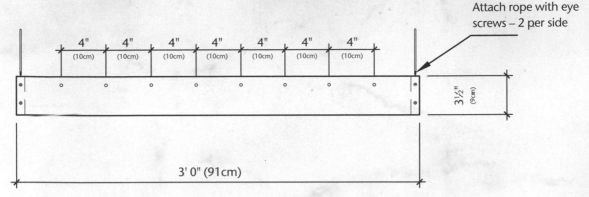

Attach rope with eye screws – 2 per side

4" (10cm) 4" (10cm) 4" (10cm) 4" (10cm) 4" (10cm) 4" (10cm) 4" (10cm)

3½" (9cm)

3' 0" (91cm)

Diagram 1: Front View

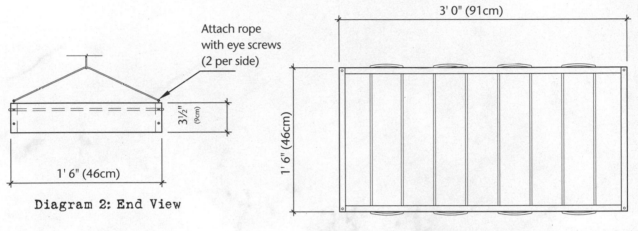

Attach rope with eye screws (2 per side)

3½" (9cm)

1' 6" (46cm)

Diagram 2: End View

3' 0" (91cm)

1' 6" (46cm)

Diagram 3: Top View

Step 1 Use a saw to cut the furring strips. You will need to cut two 3' (91cm) and two 1'6" (45cm) lengths (see Diagram 2). Pre-drill the screw holes to keep the wood from splitting. Glue and screw the corner joints together.

Step 2 Measure, mark and drill equally spaced holes along both of the long sides.

Step 3 Dilute the acrylic paint with water and brush a test sample on a piece of scrap wood. When you're pleased with the water to paint ratio, brush it onto the rack. Wipe off any drips and let it dry. Apply a protective coat of sealer over the tinted wood.

Step 4 Knot one end of the line and thread the open end down into the first hole. Stretch the line straight across to the hole in the other side of the frame. Make a stitch by bringing the line across the outside of the frame and down into the next hole. Continue working in this fashion, making straight lines across the inside of the rack and making stitches on the outside (see Diagram 2). Threading and pulling the clothesline tight works better as a two-person job.

Step 5 Attach two eye screws on, near each corner of the short boards and attach a hanging cord between each pair of screws

If your mailbox is showing signs of rust and wear, it may be time to give it a creative makeover. Covering it with old license plates not only strengthens the box, it also makes an eye-catching reflective marker for your home. In Maine, our mailbox has to survive close encounters with snowplows, and the extra illumination the license plates provide has helped protect it. My husband loved this project because it was a great excuse to buy a new (albeit inexpensive) tool—a rivet setter is a must here.

Ask your friends and neighbors for license plates. Many people save them in their garage but never use them. They'll be happy to see them put to use. Vanity plates can add a humorous touch. Very old plates are collectors items and are often high priced in flea markets and antique stores. Keep your eye out for more recent cast-offs.

License Plate Mailbox

Materials List

RECYCLED MATERIALS
Mailbox
Eight license plates

TOOLS & SUPPLIES
Drill
Rivet gun
Rivets
Tin snips

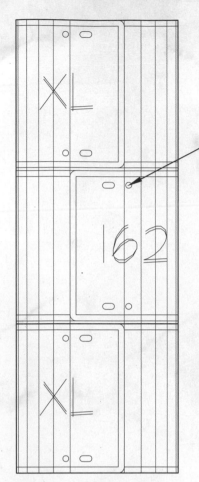

Rivet holes (2 per plate)

Diagram 1: Top View

Step 1 Unscrew the closure bar from the top of the mailbox and the lever from the front door, and carefully set them aside.

Step 2 You'll need three license plates for each side of the mailbox. Lining up the short end of the plate with the base of the box, use your hands to shape the plate to contour the box. Repeat the process to shape the remaining five plates. Drill holes as needed to accommodate the rivets. Load a rivet in the rivet gun and drive it through a corner of the first plate to permanently attach it to the box. Drive four rivets into each plate to firmly anchor them to the box.

Step 3 Use the front door and back of the box as templates to cut the two remaining plates to size. Rivet these pieces to the front and back of the box.

Step 4 Drill a hole through the plates in the top of the box so that you can reinstall the closure bar. Drill a second hole through the front door plate to reinstall the lever mechanism.

Step 5 Reinstall the box outside.

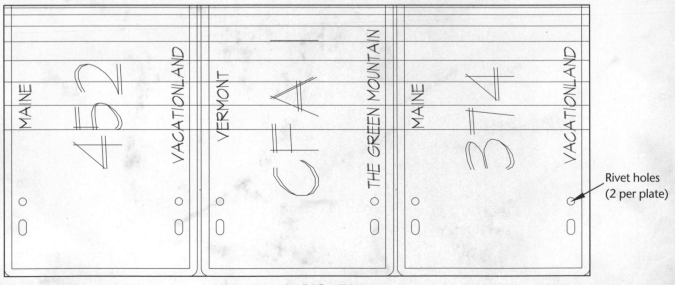

Rivet holes (2 per plate)

Diagram 2: Side View

Living the Green Life:
Ideas, Activities & Recipes

Eco Ideas

The days may be getting shorter, but there is no shortage of ways to save money and help do your part to save the environment:

o Remember that shorter days mean the lights stay on longer. Try to remember to flip the switch when you exit a room and unplug chargers when not in use. Consider borrowing a kilowatt device from your local library. It will help you determine what electronics draw the most energy in your home.

o Use compact fluorescent lightbulbs, which are proven to save electricity and money. Note: They contain hazardous chemical compounds and must be recycled appropriately. When defunct, they cannot simply go in the trash.

o Save gift bags and tins for reuse. Carefully separate gift packaging for recycling. Remove nonrecyclable parts, flatten boxes and place used wrapping paper and tissue in your recycling bin.

o Minimize air infiltration; install weather striping at doors, including the garage.

o Maximize solar heat gain; let the sun come in south-facing windows. Tile and marble floors can help collect heat during the day and slowly release it during the night, especially if there is enough thermal mass storage in the subfloor, i.e., slab on grade homes.

o Explore biodiesel alternatives and see if you can find a local drop-off center for your cooking oils.

o Check with your state and local agencies for tax incentives and rebate programs that help defer the costs of many home improvement projects which reduce energy consumption.

Relax, Unwind & Unplug

With these wintertime activities to keep you busy, there will be no time for cabin fever:

o Ski, sled and ice skate. Take in the beauty of the season.

o Read a well-loved book or visit your local library.

o Play charades, cards and dominos to get the family laughing together.

o Make candlelit ice luminaries.

o Decorate a tree with peanut butter pinecones, seed sprays and popcorn strings for the birds. Also bring them open water.

Foods for the Season

In the northeast, local fresh produce is hard to find in the winter, but this doesn't have to stop you from making delicious meals. There are fabulous dishes based on long-lasting root vegetables like sweet potatoes, onions and carrots. The fresh cranberry crops add a burst of flavor to desserts and holiday meals. Staples like homemade granola rely on dried fruits that are available anytime.

GRANOLA

This wonderful wholesome snack is another goodie from my friend Catherine. Individually wrapped bags of homemade granola make fabulous holiday gifts. I'm anxious to get a batch baking in my oven—this granola puts all prepackaged versions to shame!

½ stick butter
½ cup peanut butter
½ cup agave nectar (or honey)
4 cups rolled oats (old fashioned oatmeal)
½ cup wheat germ
1/3 cup brown sugar
¼ flour
1 teaspoon baking soda
½ cup of any (or all) of the following:
    Pecans
    Raisins
    Dried cranberries
    Chocolate chips
    Sunflower seeds
    Pumpkin seeds
    Sesame seeds
    Coconut

1. Preheat the oven to 325°F.
2. Blend the butter, peanut butter and agave nectar in a food processor.
3. Measure the dry ingredients into a large bowl and stir together.
4. Pour the butter mixture over the dry mixture and mix until well incorporated.
5. Shape the mixture into a rectangle that can be cut into bars after baking, or scatter the pieces loose on your baking sheet.
6. Bake bars for 30 minutes, or loose granola 15–20 minutes until golden.

CHICKEN NOODLE SOUP

Everyone needs to have a good chicken soup recipe on hand. This one is my favorite because the chicken cooks in the broth, enriching the soup and flavoring the meat. Nothing is better to chase away sniffles and take a bite out of the chilly air. Soup is one of the easiest meals to fix, and homemade soups lack the preservatives and salt of canned varieties. Even in the dead of winter, onions, carrots and broth are readily available.

1 onion, diced
1 carrot, quartered and diced
Celery, cut in half and sliced thin
1 tablespoon vegetable oil
1 pound boneless skinless chicken breast
2 quarts low-sodium chicken broth
Fresh thyme sprig or ¼ teaspoon dried thyme
1 bay leaf
8-ounce package wide egg noodles

1. Season the chicken with salt and pepper. Heat the oil in a Dutch oven and lightly brown the chicken over medium heat. Transfer the chicken to a plate.
2. Add the onion to the pan and cook until lightly browned. Return the chicken to the pan, along with the remaining vegetables, broth and spices. Bring the soup to a boil and then cover the pot and allow the chicken to cook through, about 10 minutes.
3. Remove the chicken to a cutting board. Add the noodles to the pot and allow them to cook until tender, about 5 minutes.
4. Meanwhile, shred the chicken with two forks. Stir the shredded chicken into the soup and serve immediately.

o o o o o o o o o o o o o o o o o o o

SWEET POTATO AND
BLACK BEAN BURRITOS

Jeanne Baker Stinson shared this easy yet incredibly delicious dish at a recipe swap party, and it's become one of my standbys. Grab sweet potatoes when the harvest comes in around Thanksgiving, then peel, grate and sauté them with black beans to make a fabulous dinner.

1 teaspoon olive oil
1 large sweet potato, peeled and grated
1 16-ounce can black beans
Tortilla shells
Monterey Jack cheese, grated
Lettuce
Sour cream
Salsa

1. Heat the oil in a skillet. Add the potato and cook, stirring occasionally, for about 10–15 minutes. Add beans and cook until heated through.
2. Warm the tortilla shells. Fill each one with the potato mixture and add some grated cheese and lettuce. Other burrito ingredients can be mixed in or served on the side, with sour cream and salsa as a dressing.

CRANBERRY SQUARES

This sweet treat is perfect for the holidays when fresh cranberries are abundant. Butter, sugar and a hint of almond complement the cranberries' tart flavor.

1½ cups sugar
2 large eggs
1½ sticks butter, melted
1 teaspoon almond extract
1½ cups flour
2 cups cranberries
½ cup chopped almonds

1. Preheat the oven to 350°F and lightly grease a 9" × 9" pan.
2. Beat the sugar and eggs until thickened. Beat in melted butter and almond extract. Add the flour and stir. Stir in the cranberries and nuts. Pour mixture into greased pan.
3. Bake for 1 hour or until a knife or toothpick inserted in the center comes out clean.

o o o o o o o o o o o o o o o o o o o

CARROT CAKE

Carrots are sweet and wonderful to bake with. This handy root vegetable keeps well all winter and plays a major role in making our family's favorite birthday cake. The recipe comes from my husband's childhood neighbor Jeanne Houlten.

3 cups grated carrot
4 eggs
2 cups sugar
1½ cups vegetable oil
2 teaspoons baking soda
½ teaspoon salt
2 teaspoons cinnamon
½ teaspoon allspice
2 cups flour
½ cup walnuts, plus more for topping

Icing
4 ounces cream cheese
¼ pound butter
½ pound powdered sugar

1. Preheat the oven to 350°F. Grease and flour two round cake pans or one 13" × 9" pan.
2. Combine the carrot, eggs, sugar and oil and mix well. Combine the baking soda, salt, cinnamon, allspice and flour and add to the wet ingredients. Grind the nuts and fold them into the batter. (We do this in the coffee grinder to enhance the flavor of the nuts.) Pour the batter into the pans and bake for 40 minutes or until a knife or toothpick inserted in the center comes out clean. Let the cake cool completely before frosting.
3. Beat together the cream cheese, butter and sugar. Spread a generous layer over the cake, and top with a sprinkling of chopped walnuts.

Resources: Knitting Techniques

Though the majority of the projects in this book are knitted with nontraditional materials, the conventional knitting techniques are used. Once you can cast on, knit, purl, decrease and bind off, you can make any of the projects in this book. Keep in mind, traditional yarn is consistent and slides easily on the needles, making it ideal to work with. If you're a true beginner, the *Blizzard Yarn Afghan* (see page 111) is a wonderful place to start, then work your way to the *Knitted Linens Rug* (see page 26) or *Knitted Plarn Tote* (see page 56).

 CAST ON This is the term used for creating the number of stitches needed for the first row of any project. It's also the most common way to cast on stitches. It might seem a little awkward to hold the yarn this way and hook the needle tip through each loop, but once you get the hang of it, you'll be amazed at how quickly the stitches add up.

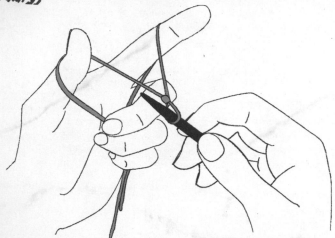

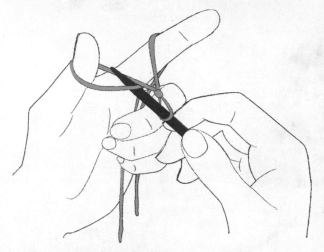

Step 1 Make a slipknot, leaving a long tail (at least 2" [5cm] for every 1" [3cm] you'll be casting on) and slide it onto the needle with the long tail dangling from the front of the needle. Slide your thumb and index finger between the two strands of yarn, and wrap the tail around your thumb and the strand still attached to the skein around your index finger. Catch both strands under your remaining fingers to provide stability.

Step 2 Bring the needle tip under the strand of yarn in front of your thumb, then over the strand behind your thumb.

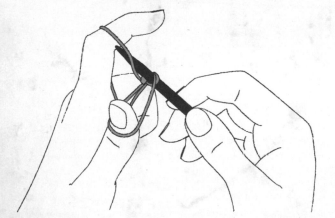

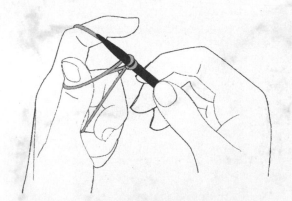

Step 3 Bring the needle behind the strand of yarn on the front of your index finger and "grab" it with the needle tip.

Step 4 Bring the yarn back through the loop you created with your thumb, creating a second loop on your needle (your first cast-on stitch). Let the loop fall away from your thumb, then tug gently on the strands with your thumb and index finger to tighten the loop. Keep your cast-on stitches on the looser side rather than tightening them excessively.

KNIT (CONTINENTAL) This technique shows you how to hold the yarn in your left hand and dip the right-hand needle into it with each stitch to avoid repetitive yarn wraps. If you're having trouble with this method, you can always hold the yarn in your right hand and manually wrap it around the needle in Step 2.

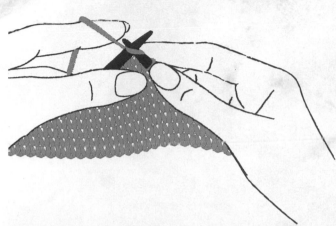

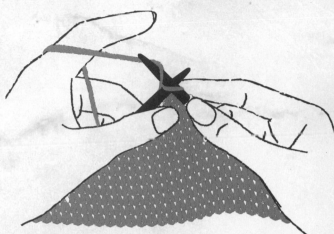

Step 1 With the yarn wrapped around or under your left index finger, insert the right needle into the first stitch on the left needle from front to back. The right-hand needle should cross behind the left-hand needle.

Step 2 Place the right needle tip behind the yarn held in your left hand. The side of the needle facing you will be wrapped in yarn. Dip the needle tip down to begin pulling it through the stitch on the left needle.

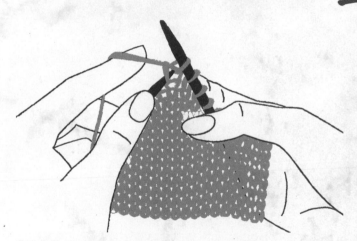

Step 3 Pull the wrapped yarn through the stitch on the left needle, and bring the yarn up on the right needle to create a new stitch, allowing the old stitch to slide easily off the left-hand needle. The new stitch remains on the right-hand needle.

Other Useful Knitting Terms

Placing a Marker: When the pattern calls for you to place a marker, this simply means sliding a plastic disk or different colored yarn loop onto the needle so it rests in between the specified stitches. Move the marker from one needle to the other when you come to it.

Garter Stitch: Garter stitch is created when you knit every single row back and forth on straight needles. It's perfect for rugs and afghans because the finished piece lays flat.

Ribbing: To create ribbing, you simply alternate between making knit and purl stitches. Ribbing creates a more elastic compact edge, and it is often used for cuffs and hat brims.

Knitting in the Round: Knitting in the round is a quick and easy way to create a tubular knitted piece, which is ideal for creating bags. Cast your stitches onto a circular needle; make sure they're not twisted. Push the stitches to the needle ends and begin knitting into the left needle. The stitches will automatically connect so that you can continue knitting around and around without interruption.

PURL (CONTINENTAL) Purling creates a raised wavy pattern, producing bumps in the front where the yarn is held and wrapped. Note the back side of a knitted row looks like a purl row, because in a knit row the yarn is wrapped at the back of the work. Conversely, the back of a purl row looks like a knit row because the yarn is wrapped in the front.

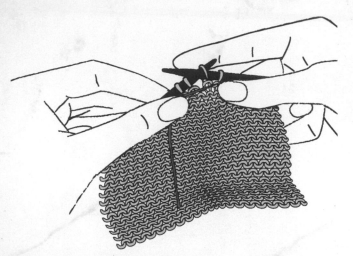

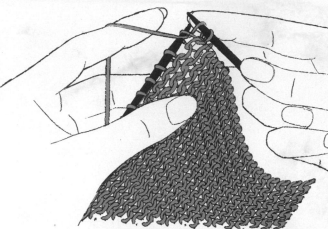

Step 1 Hold the working yarn in your left hand and situate the stitches about ½" to 1" (1cm to 3cm) away from the tips of the needles. Slide the tip of the right-hand needle into the first stitch on the left-hand needle from back to front.

Step 2 Use your left hand to wrap the working yarn around the tip of the right-hand needle counterclockwise. Draw the right-hand needle back through the stitch, catching the wrapped working yarn with the tip of the needle and bringing it back through the stitch on the left-hand needle.

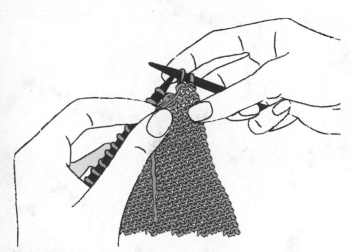

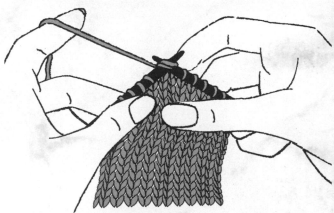

Step 3 Pull the old stitch off the left-hand needle, creating a new purl stitch on the right-hand needle. For illustration purposes, the working yarn is shown held between the index finger and thumb. However, when working an entire row without stopping, the yarn should remain in the position shown in Step 2 to create proper tension.

Decrease/Knit Two Together Decreasing, or eliminating stitches, makes a piece smaller. To knit two together, place your needle tip through two stitches instead of one, knitting the stitches together in a single stitch.

Slide the right-hand needle (from front to back, as for a regular knit stitch) into two stitches together, and knit them together as one stitch. This decreases one stitch.

BIND OFF Binding off is the technique of looping one stitch into another, stabilizing the edge of your work so the stitches do not unravel. Be careful not to pull the stitches too tightly when you bind off. If your tension is too tight, you'll pucker the edge of your work.

Step 1 Knit the first two stitches in the row just as you would for a normal knitted row.

Step 2 Insert the left-hand needle into the first knitted stitch and pass that stitch over the second knitted stitch.

Step 3 There is now one less stitch on the right-hand needle.

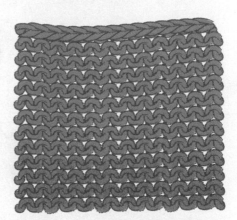

Step 4 To bind off the next stitch, knit one more stitch (two stitches are now on the right-hand needle), then pass the preceding stitch over that one. Continue to knit one stitch and then pass the preceding stitch over it until you have bound off all the stitches. Cut the yarn and pull the tail through the final stitch.

Resources: Crochet Techniques

All the crochet projects in this book—*Fruit Net Pot Scrubbers* (see page 25), *T-Shirt Frisbee* (see page 50) and *Raffia Garlic Dryer* (see page 94) are circular. You start them by making a few links of chain and then hooking the needle back through the first stitch to turn the straight chain links into a loop.

Once you've made a loop, follow the directions to make either single or double crochet stitches through the center of the loop. Once you've made the required number of stitches into the center of the loop, push your hook back through your first stitch to complete the circle. From this point on you're ready to crochet directly into the top of each stitch as shown in the following diagrams.

CHAIN STITCH The chain is the first step of any crochet project. It's also just like a single knitted stitch that grows with every new loop of yarn.

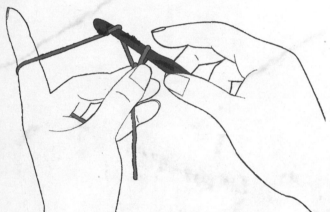

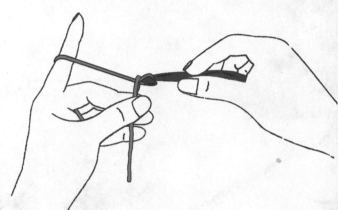

Step 1 Make a slipknot at the free end of the yarn (the other end will be attached to the skein/ball). Slide the slipknot onto a crochet hook, then wrap the working yarn around the back of the hook clockwise.

Step 2 Move the hook so it grabs the wrapped working yarn, then pull the working yarn through the slipknot to form the first chain stitch.

Step 3 Continue to wrap the working yarn and pull it through each subsequent loop until the chain is the desired length.

SINGLE CROCHET This type of stitch makes a neat row of compact stitches. If you're just beginning your work, you'll need to prepare a crochet chain or loop before making your first single crochet stitch.

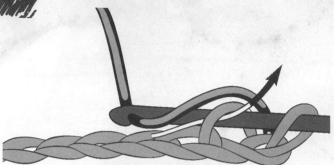

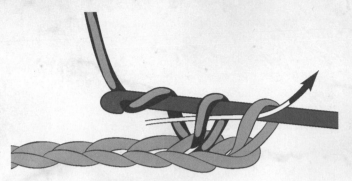

Step 1 To begin the single crochet stitch, pass your hook through the closest stitch in the chain or the center of the loop. Wrap the yarn from front to back around the needle. Bring the hooked yarn back up through the stitch.

Step 2 You should have two loops left on your hook. Wrap the yarn around the hook again and bring the yarn up through both loops. This completes your first single crochet stitch.

DOUBLE CROCHET The double crochet stitch is taller with a more lacey appearance. If you're just beginning your work, you'll need to prepare a crochet chain or loop before making your first double crochet stitch.

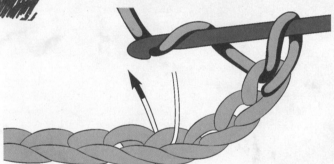

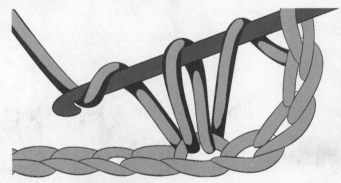

Step 1 Start by wrapping the yarn front to back around the hook. Keep it wrapped while you pass the hook through the closest chain or center of the loop.

Step 2 Wrap the yarn around the hook and bring it back up through the stitch. You'll now have three loops on your hook. Wrap the yarn around the hook again and bring it through the next two loops closest to the hook end.

Step 3 Wrap the yarn around the hook a final time and bring it through the two remaining loops. This completes your first double crochet stitch.

Resources: Embroidery Techniques

The decorative stitches in this book are made with a full strand of embroidery floss. Using embroidery floss creates highly visible stitches, even when made on top of heavy denim and recycled sweater pieces. These simple stitches are a great introduction to the art of embroidery.

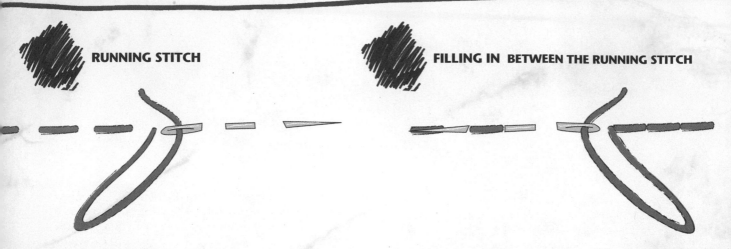

RUNNING STITCH

FILLING IN BETWEEN THE RUNNING STITCH

This is the first hand sewing stitch. The needle goes in and out, up and down through the fabric at regular intervals to make even stitches. This stitch is used to sew two pieces of fabric together or to make a straight decorative line.

Draw the needle up through the underside of the fabric so that the knot rests against the back side of your work. Poke the needle in and out of the fabric to make two or three stitches at a time. Pull the needle all the way up so that any slack is removed from the thread. You'll have instantly made two or three stitches. Repeat the process until you've stitched the desired length. Knot the thread on the underside of the work or turn the needle around to fill the spaces between stitches (see *Filling in Between the Running Stitch*, to the right).

To make the bird designs on the *Denim Quilt* (page 30), I filled in the spaces between stitches with a second running stitch. Some people prefer to use a backstitch to make a solid line, but I think this is just as easy and works the thread back down to the starting point so that you can stitch other elements of the design.

Draw the needle up through the beginning of the last stitch. Thread the needle up and down between the last couple of stitches to completely fill the blank spaces between them. Pull the needle and thread up to remove any slack. Repeat the process until you've created new stitches between the running stitches. Knot the thread on the back side of the fabric.

WHIPSTITCH

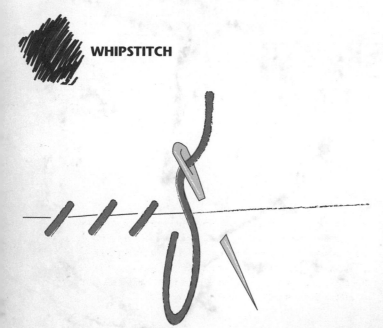

Like the running stitch, a whipstitch can be functional or decorative. It commonly serves both purposes at once, decoratively joining two overlapping pieces of fabric. The needle goes up and down through the fabric to make single parallel stitches. It requires a little more time than the running stitch, as you can't line up multiple stitches on your needle.

Draw the needle up through the underside of your work so that the knot rests against the back side of your work. Thread the needle back down at an angle from where you first pulled it up. Repeat the process, trying to keep the stitches the same length and angled in the same direction. Note: If you were to reverse directions and fill in this stitch, it would make a zigzag.

FRENCH KNOT

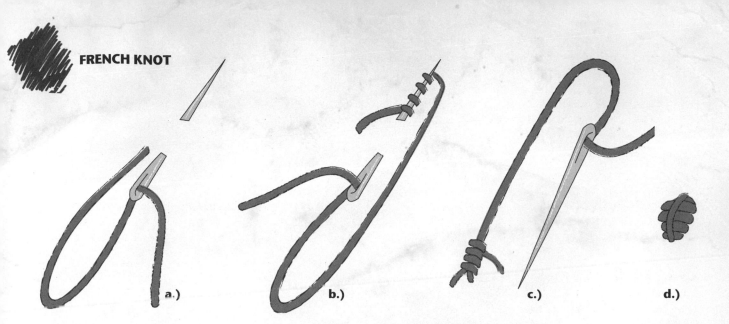

a.)   b.)   c.)   d.)

The French knot is a clever way to make eyes and flower centers. It's a knot that sits on top of the fabric exactly where you need it. I've intentionally simplified the technique for my benefit as well as yours. **a.)** Draw the needle up through the fabric where you need the knot to show. Push the needle through the fabric to catch a small amount on the needle (just like the first stitch in the running stitch). **b.)** Wrap the base of the thread (where it first emerged from the fabric) four times around the needle point. **c.)** Pull the needle point straight up through the looped thread. If necessary, slide the loops down against the fabric. To finish the stitch, simply poke the needle back down beside where it came up in the first step. **d.)** When you pull the excess thread taut your French knot should sit on top of the fabric.

LEAF OR FLOWER PETAL

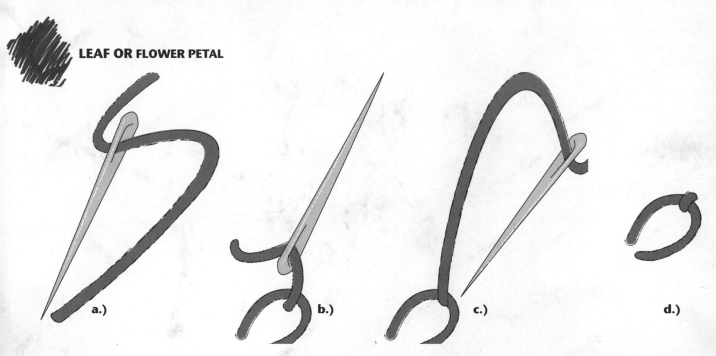

a.)   b.)   c.)   d.)

This stitch requires two steps: The first stitch is a very loose loop, and the second stitch holds the center of the loop in a flower or leaf shape. Four or five of these stitches placed together make a fabulous flower. One or two alongside a running stitch stem make great leaves. **a.)** Draw the needle up where you want the base of the leaf or flower to be. Bring the needle back down next to where it came out. Be careful not to pull the thread tight. Position the loose thread how you'd like your finished leaf or petal to look. The more loose thread you leave in the stitch, the bigger your finished leaf or flower will be; conversely, the less thread you leave, the smaller they will be. **b.)** Bring the needle back up on the inside center of the loop. **c.)** Bring the needle back down on the outside center of the loop leaf/petal shape. **d.)** This should make a tiny stitch that traps the first stitch in place.

Resources: Materials

BEADALON (www.beadalon.com)
Rubber tubing, cabled stringing wire, Supple-max, Beadfix glue, jewelry-making tools

BLUE MOON BEADS
(www.creativityinc.com)
Beads and jewelry supplies

CLOVER (www.clover-usa.com)
Felting needles and wool roving supplies, knitting and crochet needles

CRYSTALLIZED SWAROVSKI ELEMENTS
(www.create-your-style.com)
Rhinestones

DECOART (www.decoart.com)
Liquid Beadz glue

DMC (www.dmc-usa.com)
Sewing and embroidery threads

DUNCAN (www.ilovetocreate.com)
Aleene's 7800 All-Purpose Adhesive, Aleene's Platinum Bond Glass and Bead Adhesive, Aleene's Tacky Glue

FAMOWOOD
(www.eclecticproducts.com)
Cast resin solution

FISKARS (www.fiskars.com)
Paper trimmer, softouch scissors

PLAID (www.plaidonline.com)
Glass rings, Mod Podge, Make-It Mosaics tile cutter, adhesive and sealer

PRYM-DRITZ (www.dritz.com)
Purse handles

NATURE-FIL (www.poly-fil.com)
Bamboo stuffing

RANGER INDUSTRIES
(www.rangerink.com)
Glossy Accents

JCA, INC. (www.jcacrafts.com)
Blizzard yarn

THERM O WEB
(www.thermoweb.com)
Heat N' Bond iron-on adhesive

TONER PLASTICS
(www.tonercrafts.com)
Fun Wire

Resources: Patterns

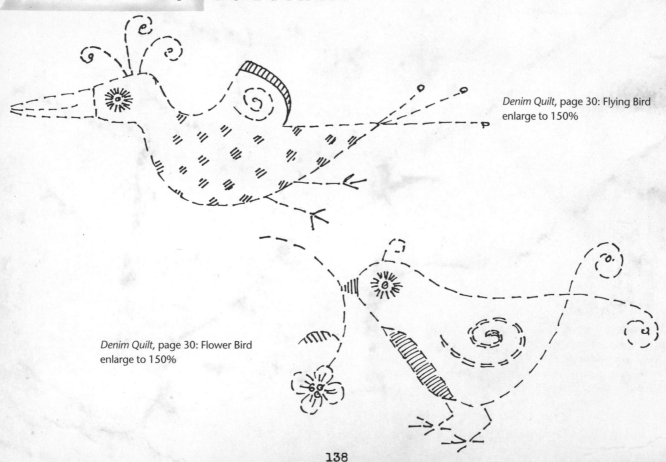

Denim Quilt, page 30: Flying Bird
enlarge to 150%

Denim Quilt, page 30: Flower Bird
enlarge to 150%

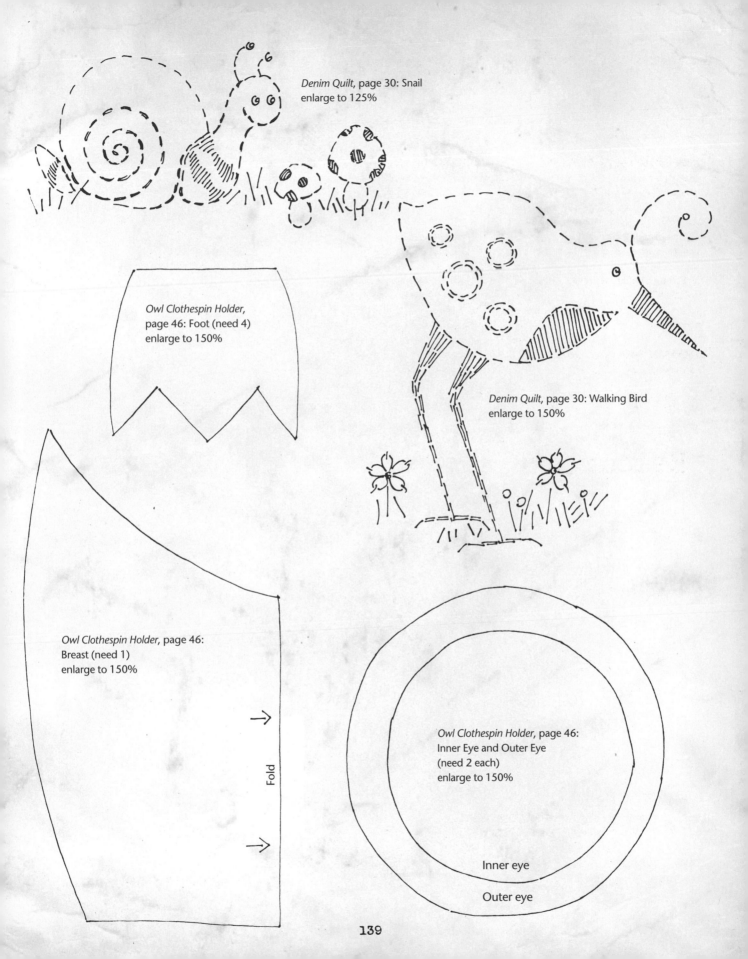

Denim Quilt, page 30: Snail
enlarge to 125%

Owl Clothespin Holder,
page 46: Foot (need 4)
enlarge to 150%

Denim Quilt, page 30: Walking Bird
enlarge to 150%

Owl Clothespin Holder, page 46:
Breast (need 1)
enlarge to 150%

Fold

Owl Clothespin Holder, page 46:
Inner Eye and Outer Eye
(need 2 each)
enlarge to 150%

Inner eye

Outer eye

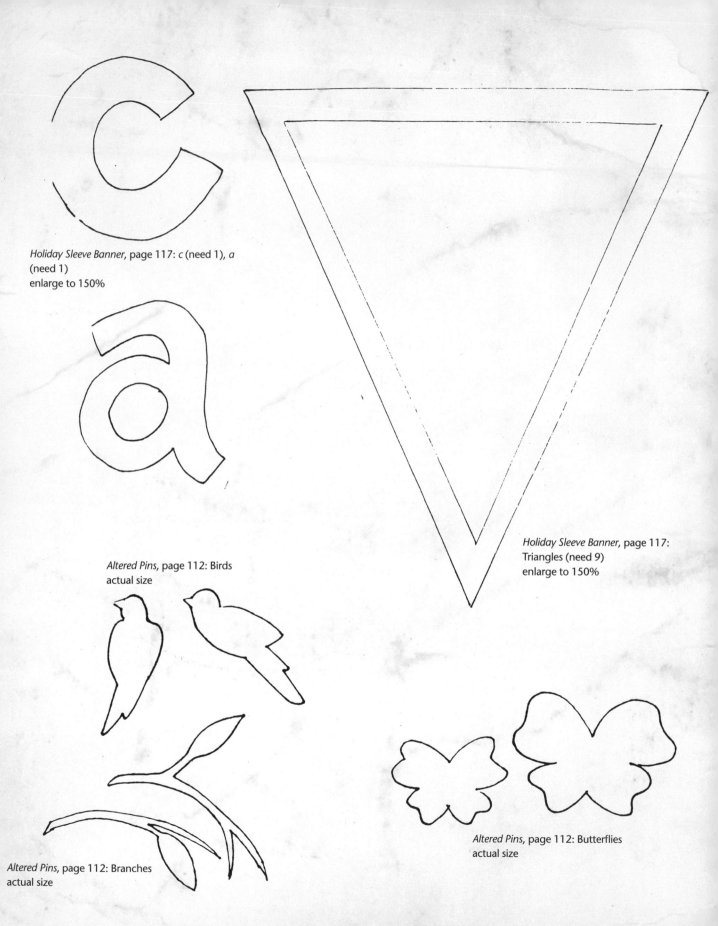

Holiday Sleeve Banner, page 117: *c* (need 1), *a* (need 1)
enlarge to 150%

Holiday Sleeve Banner, page 117: Triangles (need 9)
enlarge to 150%

Altered Pins, page 112: Birds
actual size

Altered Pins, page 112: Branches
actual size

Altered Pins, page 112: Butterflies
actual size

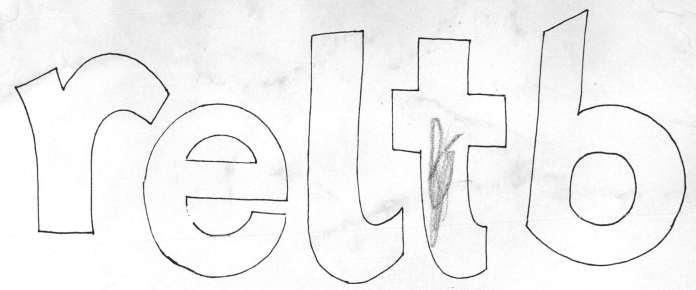

Holiday Sleeve Banner, page 117: *r* (need 1), *e* (need 3), *l* (need 1), *t* (need 1), *b* (need 1) enlarge each letter to 150%

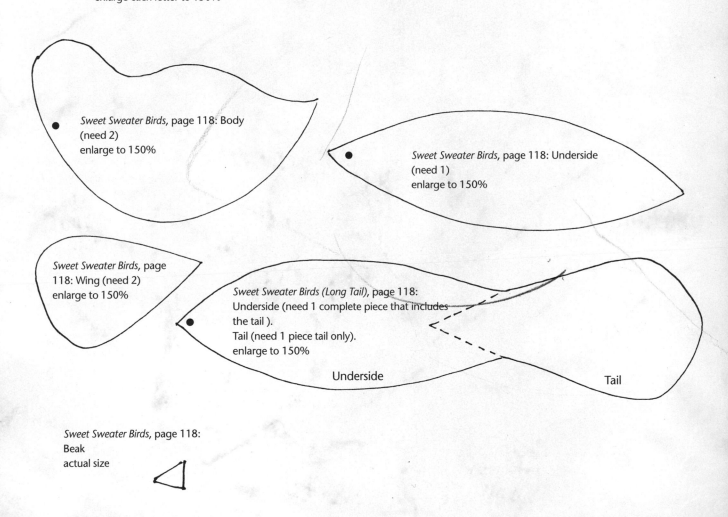

Sweet Sweater Birds, page 118: Body (need 2) enlarge to 150%

Sweet Sweater Birds, page 118: Underside (need 1) enlarge to 150%

Sweet Sweater Birds, page 118: Wing (need 2) enlarge to 150%

Sweet Sweater Birds (Long Tail), page 118: Underside (need 1 complete piece that includes the tail). Tail (need 1 piece tail only). enlarge to 150%

Underside

Tail

Sweet Sweater Birds, page 118: Beak actual size

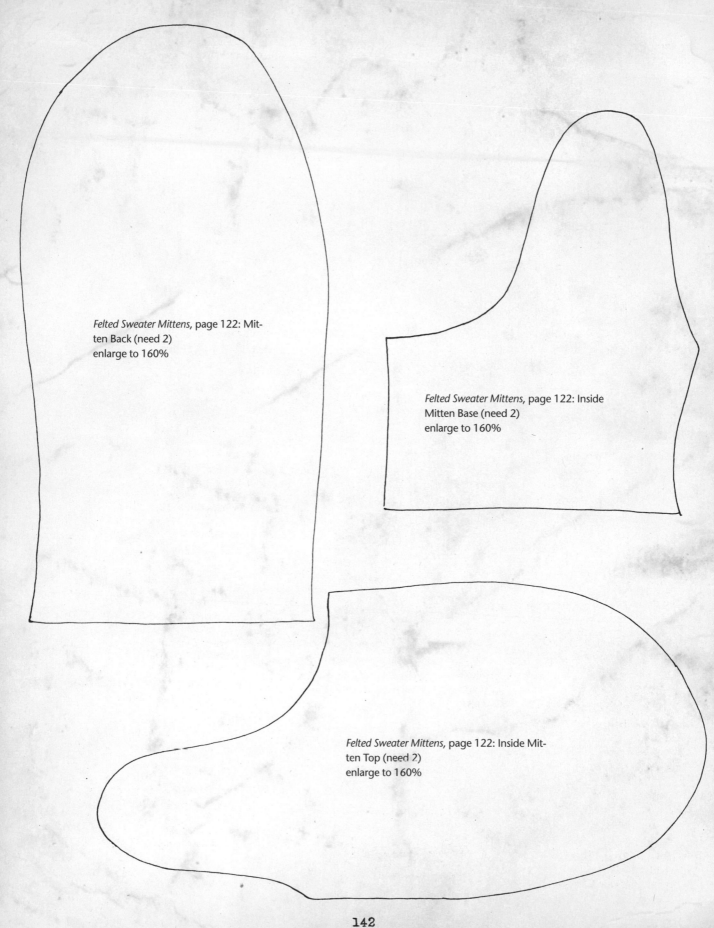

Felted Sweater Mittens, page 122: Mitten Back (need 2)
enlarge to 160%

Felted Sweater Mittens, page 122: Inside Mitten Base (need 2)
enlarge to 160%

Felted Sweater Mittens, page 122: Inside Mitten Top (need 2)
enlarge to 160%

Index

Even more ways to craft a better life!

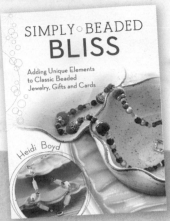

Simply Beaded Bliss

By Heidi Boyd

Features 40+ step-by-step beaded projects, including jewelry, gifts and cards that feature dynamic mixed-media elements such as polymer clay, scrapbook embellishments, sequins, wire, lightweight materials and more!

ISBN-13: 978-1-60061-095-0
ISBN-10: 1-60061-095-1
8¼ x 10⅞ paperback, 144 pages, Z2004

Soft + Simple Knits for Little Ones

By Heidi Boyd

Features basic techniques section, plus 45 quick-and-easy patterns to make for babies and toddlers, including clothing, toys and accessories!

ISBN-13: 978-1-58180-965-7
ISBN-10: 1-58180-965-4
8 x 8 paperback, 160 pages, Z0696

Warm Fuzzies

By Betz White

Techniques, tips and patterns for creating 30 deliciously cute felted items, including delectable pillows and throws as well as tasty hats, scarves, pincushions and handbags.

ISBN-13: 978-1-60061-007-3
ISBN-10: 1-60061-007-2
8½ x 11 paperback with flaps, 144 pages, Z1026

Practically Green

By Micaela Preston

Take the practical approach to living mindfully! Includes 20+ green projects—from green body care products to re-crafted sewing projects—as well as copy-and-clip guides for eco-friendly shopping and healthy recipes to replace packaged convenience snacks.

ISBN-13: 978-1-60061-329-6
ISBN-10: 1-60061-329-2
5¼ x 7 paperback with flaps, 224 pages, Z2972

3 1901 04367 8061

These books and other fine North Light books are available at your local bookstore or online supplier.
Or visit our Web site, **www.mycraftivity.com**.